FabJob Guide to

Become a
Landscape
Company Owner

JANET HARTIN

FABJOB® GUIDE TO BECOME A
LANDSCAPE COMPANY OWNER
by Janet Hartin
Edited by Jennifer James

ISBN: 978-1-894638-96-8

Library and Archives Canada Cataloguing in Publication

Hartin, Janet
FabJob guide to become a landscape company owner / by Janet Hartin; edited by Jennifer James.

Includes bibliographical references.
ISBN 978-1-894638-96-8

1. Landscaping industry--Management. 2. Landscape gardening--Vocational guidance. 3. New business enterprises. I. James, Jennifer II. Title. III. Title: Become a landscape company owner.

SB472.5.H37 2006   712.068   C2006-901413-2

Important Disclaimer: Although every effort has been made to ensure this guide is free from errors, this publication is sold with the understanding that the authors, editors, and publisher are not responsible for the results of any action taken on the basis of information in this work, nor for any errors or omissions. The publishers, and the authors and editors, expressly disclaim all and any liability to any person, whether a purchaser of this publication or not, in respect of anything and of the consequences of anything done or omitted to be done by any such person in reliance, whether whole or partial, upon the whole or any part of the contents of this publication. If expert advice is required, services of a competent professional person should be sought.

About the Websites Mentioned in this Guide: Although we aim to provide the information you need within the guide, we have also included a number of websites because readers have told us they appreciate knowing about sources of additional information. (**TIP:** Don't include a period at the end of a web address when you type it into your browser.) Due to the constant development of the Internet, websites can change. Any websites mentioned in this guide are included for the convenience of readers only. We are not responsible for the content of any sites except FabJob.com.

FabJob Inc.
19 Horizon View Court
Calgary, Alberta, Canada T3Z 3M5

FabJob Inc.
4616 25th Avenue NE, #224
Seattle, Washington, USA 98105

To order books in bulk, phone 403-949-2039
To arrange a media interview, phone 403-949-4980

www.FabJob.com
THE DREAM CAREER EXPERTS

Contents

1. Introduction 1

   1.1 Landscaping as a Profession..2

      1.1.1 Types of Jobs...3

      1.1.2 Landscaping Specialties 6

      1.1.3 The Landscaping Market.......................................7

      1.1.4 Benefits of the Career 8

   1.2 Inside this Guide 11

2. How to Do the Job 13

   2.1 Botany Basics...13

      2.1.1 Plants and Water...14

      2.1.2 Nutrients and Fertilizers......................................20

      2.1.3 You've Got Weeds..23

      2.1.4 Common Plant Troubles.......................................24

      2.1.5 Environmentally Friendly Landscapes 25

   2.2 Assessing Clients' Needs...27

      2.2.1 The Initial Meeting 28

      2.2.2 An Onsite Survey...29

      2.2.3 Landscape Design..30

      2.2.4 Timelines and Proposals......................................32

      2.2.5 Client Contracts 34

   2.3 Planting and Maintaining Turf 35

      2.3.1 Turf Irrigation...38

      2.3.2 Thatch and Soil Compaction................................40

      2.3.3 Fertilization 41

      2.3.4 Mowing the Grass 43

      2.3.5 Common Turf Problems.......................................49

About the Author

 Janet Hartin has had a love for plants and nature as far back as she can remember. Her early enthusiasm was spawned by family vacations to nearly every national park in the United States by the time she was 16. Her first paid horticulture job was selling nursery and bedding plants at a Midwest retail nursery, followed by a move to Hilo, Hawaii where she worked in the anthurium industry. After a year in paradise (and a 7.1 earthquake!) she moved to Minnesota where she obtained B.S. and M.S. degrees in horticulture from the University of Minnesota.

During college, Janet continued to work in the horticulture industry in both the public and private landscape sectors. Keeping in touch with real-world problems, opportunities, and advancements in the world of horticulture, coupled with her education, helped land Janet her dream job in 1984 as a horticulturist with the University of California Cooperative Extension, a position she still holds. Her position allows her to work directly with the landscape industry, keeping people at all stages of their careers abreast of the latest research-based information on plant varieties, irrigation and pest management techniques, and tree, shrub, and turf care. She has published more than 100 articles, fact sheets, technical publications and books on horticulture topics, and presented hundreds of talks to industry and professional societal groups, both nationally and internationally.

Janet lives with her teenage daughter Stephanie (who aspires to be a professional ballerina rather than a horticulturist) in southern California and is engaged to Joe, a psychology professor/associate dean. In her spare time, she enjoys — you guessed it — gardening, hiking, camping, and kayaking.

About the Editor

 Jennifer James is a leading writer and editor of career and business guides. She has written, edited, and contributed to more than 50 books about breaking into all sorts of desirable careers, including the *FabJob Guide to Become a Wedding Planner*, the *FabJob Guide to Become a Caterer or Personal Chef*, and the Amazon bestseller *Dream Careers* by Tag and Catherine Goulet. In addition to writing about fabulous careers, Jennifer has one herself: she is a public relations and special events coordinator for a successful craft brewery.

Acknowledgments

I would like to thank the following landscape industry professionals for offering invaluable tips and suggestions for those pursuing careers as landscape company owners in North America. They are all well respected and highly successful in their respective specialties, and their advice is deeply appreciated and should take you far in pursuing your personal goals.

Special gratitude is extended to Dan Foley, President of Professional Landcare Network (PLANET, formerly ALCA), and David Zoldoske, President of the Irrigation Association (IA) for taking time from their extraordinarily busy schedules to offer expert advice to readers of the *FabJob Guide to Become a Landscape Company Owner*.

- *Debra Amerson*
  Plantris Productions
  Marin County, California

- *Bill Baker*
  William Baker & Associates
  Temecula, California

- *Mark Borst*
  Borst Landscape and Design
  Allentown, New Jersey

- *Peter Brown*
  Real Green Systems
  Walled Lake, Michigan

- *Donna Burdick*
  D&J Landscape Contractors
  Portland, Oregon

- *Carl Clifton*
  Lawnscape, Inc.
  Montclair, California

- *Dan Foley*
  President, Professional Landcare
  Network (PLANET), and
  President, Foley Landscape, Inc.
  South Walpole, Massachusetts

- *Tom Heaviland*
  Heaviland Enterprises, Inc.
  Vista, California

- *Dr. David Hensley*
  University of Arkansas
  Fayetteville, Arkansas

- *Peter Hincks*
  Timberwolf Corporation
  Rutland, Vermont

- *Dr. Ed Gilman*
  University of Florida
  Gainesville, Florida

- *Doug Jacobs*
  AA Equipment
  Montclair, California

- *Ken LaVoie III*
  LaVoie Landscape Management
  Winslow, Maine

- *Sharon Lilly*
  International Society of
  Arboriculture
  Champaign, Illinois

- *Charles Mann*
  Charles Mann Photography
  Santa Fe, New Mexico

- *Brad Woodford*
  Bradley Landscape Development, Inc.
  Encinitas, California

- *Dr. David Zoldoske*
  Irrigation Association (IA), Falls Church, Virginia and California State University, Fresno, California

In addition, I would like to express appreciation to the FabJob team of professionals for the opportunity to write this career guide. Especially, I am indebted to Jen James for editing the manuscript and offering valuable content suggestions.

1. Introduction

Think back to some of your fondest childhood memories. Chances are they include playing an outdoor sport such as baseball, chasing fireflies through the grass, climbing trees, lying on your back in a park watching the clouds, or smelling freshly cut roses from your backyard. Mine sure do.

I've always loved exploring nature and have been in awe of it as far back as I can remember. That's why I chose the career I'm in, and likely why you're reading this book about starting up your own landscape company.

Landscaping involves the art and science of planting and caring for trees, shrubs, groundcovers, flowers and turf, in both formal and informal settings. It also includes non-living components, such as patios, walkways, barbecues, decks, walks, retaining walls, lighting, statuary and anything else external to the house.

The rewards of landscaping can be appreciated now and by future generations in gardens, backyards, parks and schoolyards around the world. Just imagine your neighborhood void of trees and other plants. Plants add endless joy and beauty to our lives.

Besides beautifying a setting and keeping us alive by providing oxygen, landscape plants produce shade, reduce noise, improve water quality, provide food and shelter for wildlife, reduce street glare, buffer temperature, minimize erosion, and provide cushioning for sports. They can also have a calming effect on people and can reduce stress.

There's never been a better time than now to delve into this rewarding profession. If you want a job that allows you to fully appreciate nature, becoming a landscape company owner is an ideal career. Developing your skills as a landscaper is a dream you can realize without getting a college degree. What it does require is a vision, learning a lot about plants from books and real-world experience, excellent people skills, and a solid business plan. I have attempted to make this career guide a comprehensive resource for all those things.

Congratulations on taking the first step in choosing a healthy, environmentally friendly career that can bring you happiness, job satisfaction, independence, and financial freedom! Following the suggestions in this career guide will help make your dream become a reality.

1.1   Landscaping as a Profession

Professional landscapers do all sorts of things, so there are many career paths to choose from in this profession. Whether you're interested in being a generalist who works in all areas, or a specialist with a landscaping niche, there's a great career awaiting you. Some typical projects that landscapers design, install and/or maintain include:

- Residential yards and estates

- Public and private school grounds

- Public parks, recreation sites, and streetscapes

- Civic center landscapes and waterfronts

- Business courtyards

- Golf courses

Your key to long-term success is getting lots of experience in the plant and business end of things, developing strong skills in the area or areas you decide to pursue, obtaining necessary training and licenses, and, most of all, doing a professional job and earning the trust and respect of your clients.

In Chapter 3, I'll cover the importance of preparing yourself for a landscaping career by reading trade magazines, Cooperative Extension publications, and a few good horticulture and business books. I'll also walk you through planning your business, and discuss opportunities for obtaining training and credentials in and out of the classroom.

Several resources that are instantly accessible online or available by making a single phone call will be listed, along with references for obtaining high-quality certifications that will increase your skills and expertise and raise the respect your customers have for you.

1.1.1   Types of Jobs

Here are some of the areas of expertise within the landscaping profession. You may specialize in one or more of these areas yourself, or you may work with these people as fellow contractors or employees.

Landscape Maintenance Personnel (Gardeners)

These people care for and protect the beauty of established landscapes. They provide services such as mowing, fertilizing, irrigating, shaping and pruning, and fall clean up. This is a great way to break into the profession, and you don't need a license if you stay away from working with pesticides. In fact, you can earn a very decent living in the maintenance end of things by concentrating in an area that you really like and becoming good at it.

This is an area with great potential for developing your own specialty. You can maintain your freedom by being your own boss and get paid for being outdoors and doing something you love.

Landscape Contractors

Landscape contractors construct, install and sometimes maintain (or subcontract) public and private gardens and landscapes. They often have excellent reputations as designers, as well, and, by law, must also install anything they design. Besides selecting and planting trees, shrubs, groundcovers, flowers, and turf, some also do concrete and construction work, install and repair irrigation systems and provide arboriculture (tree and shrub care) services.

In most states, landscape contractors need to be licensed, which requires three or four years of experience and passing an exam. A college degree isn't required, but some states allow applicants to substitute technical training, an apprenticeship, or education for a portion of the practical experience. Most states also require landscape contractors to be bonded and fully insured, which protects everyone.

Landscape Designers

Landscape designers create residential landscapes and can convert homeowner's visions and dreams into reality. They are not licensed landscape architects, and are not required to have a degree in landscape architecture. They may also choose to install and maintain the landscapes they design, or work with specialists and subcontractors in these areas. Many landscape designers enjoy the benefits of seeing a project from start to finish, installing and maintaining the residential designs they created.

In most states, landscape designers are limited to making plans or drawings for the selection, placement, or use of plants when the execution of the plans or drawings does not affect public health, safety or welfare.

Landscape Architects

Landscape architects design but do not install or maintain residential and large-scale private and public landscapes, irrigation systems, decks, lighting systems, and even toxic waste sites. You name it. They design just about anything related to the outdoors. In fact, the largest employer in the world of landscape architects is the U.S. National Park Service.

Landscape architects are required to be licensed in most states, and qualify to take the accompanying exam through a combination of college coursework and experience. This varies from state to state.

If you find you have a talent for landscape design, you can make a very good living as a landscape architect. The good news is, the time you've spent as a landscaper applies toward your eligibility to take the landscape architecture exam. If, however, you don't like the design end of things, you can choose another segment of the landscape industry, such as arboriculture or a maintenance specialty.

Greenskeepers and Golf Course Superintendents

Greenskeepers maintain turf and other plantings grown on private and public golf courses. They handle irrigation, fertilization, aeration, and sometimes pest management (if they have a license), and are usually very familiar with a wide array of equipment. In the Western U.S. they may be well versed in irrigation systems or work closely with a licensed specialist, and may or may not be in charge of tree care. They work for golf course superintendents, who have the ultimate responsibility for keeping the golf course healthy and attractive.

Golf course superintendents usually have four-year college degrees, but not always. Many started out as assistant golf course superintendents or even as greenskeepers and worked their way up. They may hold many licenses themselves, or hire/contract specialists in arboriculture, irrigation and pest management who do.

Arborists

Arborists are tree care specialists. They are trained and experienced in pruning, fertilization, irrigation, and tree planting, and can often diagnosis and treat pest problems, as well.

Most states require arborists to have a contractor's license, and the International Society of Arboriculture (**www.isa-arbor.com**) offers an excellent voluntary certification program for arborists through verification of experience, testing and continuing education requirements. ISA Certified Arborists, for example, have a minimum of three years experience in tree care and have passed a comprehensive exam. Some Certified Arborists choose to receive additional training and become Municipal or Utility Specialists.

1.1.2   Landscaping Specialties

Landscapers are talented, creative professionals, often with unique skills. In fact, there are more specialty areas today than ever before and with more and more homeowners hiring professional landscapers, you don't have to worry about the market being saturated.

Within the industry, there are many specialties, such as:

- Drought-resistant landscapes
- Native landscapes
- Sustainable landscapes
- Heritage gardens
- Tree care
- Lawn care
- Sports turf maintenance
- Rooftop gardens
- Outdoor lighting
- Patios, barbecues, playgrounds
- Water features

One of the attractions of the profession is the unique ability you have as an artisan to create masterpieces that are truly your own handiwork. If you do decide to specialize, selecting the right area can greatly add to the enjoyment of your career and your overall job satisfaction.

A good example of an area that's quickly gaining momentum is sustainable landscaping. These low-input landscapes take advantage of low-water use plants that require little fertilizer, maintenance, and pesticides. Often they feature native trees, shrubs and ornamental grasses and no traditional lawn (or just a small one). Practices such as grasscycling (leaving lawn clippings on the grass while it's mowed so they don't end up in a landfill) and composting are common in these landscapes. Since the whole idea is to grow healthy plants that don't require pesticides, you don't need to worry about being around chemicals if you have concerns about their safety and risks. And, since you won't be recommending or applying chemicals, you don't need a license.

A niche market that goes hand in hand with sustainable landscaping, especially in arid regions, is native and drought-resistant landscaping. Many homeowners in the west are interested in saving water in their landscapes to benefit the environment and to save money. They often need help choosing the right plants, planting and maintaining them, and setting up the irrigation system.

Becoming a specialist in irrigation and hydrozoning (placing plants with similar water needs together so they can be watered with the same valve) is a booming market. If you're interested in this area and eager to learn how to install and maintain irrigation systems and set up watering schedules for plants, you'll likely find lots of work and can take pride in knowing that your efforts are conserving a valuable resource.

There are many more specialty areas, as well. Do you live in an area where the biggest problem in the landscape is hungry deer? Consider starting a company specializing in deer-resistant landscaping. Do you have a knack for electrical engineering and love lighting? Become a landscape lighting specialist. Have you been on the roof of a skyscraper lately? Environmentally friendly rooftop gardens are popping up on top of prestigious buildings in cities like Chicago, Toronto and Seattle. The sky's the limit!

1.1.3   The Landscaping Market

Is there a market for your landscaping company? Yes! Beautiful formal and informal landscapes are becoming increasingly important to busy North American homeowners who have limited time to perform their own maintenance.

The U.S. Bureau of Labor Statistics' 2008 figures are also indicating that the demand for landscaping and groundskeeping services will grow faster than the national average for all occupations through 2016. They cite the following reasons, among others:

- Many two-income households lack the time to take care of their lawn

- There is a growing interest by homeowners in their backyards

- Newer homes having more and bigger windows overlooking the yard

- As the population ages, elderly homeowners will require lawn care services

- There is expected growth in the construction of all types of buildings

- Owners of many buildings and facilities recognize the importance of "curb appeal" in attracting business

A 2006 survey conducted by the National Gardening Association reported that consumers spent $45 billion in that year on professional landscape, lawn and tree care services, an increase of more than 80% over consumer spending on these services in 2001.And the American Landscape Contractors Association (now PLANET) reported that investing in landscape design and installation had more than tripled over five years, reaching $14.3 billion in 2002.

According to the U.S. Department of Labor, the number of jobs for landscapers and groundskeepers in the United States is expected to grow 18% between 2006 and 2016. This is due to a projected increased need in both the residential and commercial sector, for the reasons explained above. It's true that landscaping work is seasonal for the most part, but as you'll read later in this guide, landscape company owners have developed a number of lucrative ways to keep busy when the snow flies or things turn cold.

1.1.4   Benefits of the Career

Owning your own landscape company will let you maintain your freedom and carve your own path. The best part is you get paid for being outdoors and doing something you love! You're only limited by your own imagination.

Hands-on Outdoors Work

Do you enjoy spending time outdoors, marvel at the wonders and beauty of nature, and value a healthy, enriching lifestyle? If so, owning your own landscape company might be the perfect career choice for you.

The landscaping profession offers numerous health and psychological benefits as well. Regular physical activity improves endurance, flexibility and strength, and can reduce the risk of heart disease, obesity, high blood pressure, and cancer. Working outdoors benefits you emotionally too, increasing feelings of well-being and connectedness, and can even ward off depression.

Help the Environment

You may be drawn to this career due to the satisfaction that comes from enhancing the beauty and health of our physical environment. As mentioned earlier, landscape plants provide oxygen, conserve energy, preserve water quality, stabilize soil, improve air quality, buffer noise, and provide a habitat for birds and wildlife. For example, a single tree can remove 26 pounds of carbon dioxide from the atmosphere annually, equaling 11,000 miles of car emissions!

Homeowners are becoming more environmentally conscientious, as well, realizing the importance of landscaping with water-efficient plants, recycling greenwaste, grasscycling, and reducing reliance on pesticides. They often seek out landscapers who share their vision.

The traditional image of a private landscaper applying chemical pesticides as a mainstay is no longer valid. Today, landscapers are much more likely to utilize environmentally friendly integrated pest management strategies favoring prevention, which has resulted in a much safer environment. This is great news for you in your new career, as well as for your grandchildren.

Job Satisfaction

Job satisfaction in your new career is likely to be quite high. More than 70% of respondents in *Landscape Magazine*'s 2003 State of the Industry survey reported that they were "well rewarded" and "very" or "mostly" satisfied in their career in professional landscape management, while only 2% reported being "not satisfied or well rewarded." This sure beats the odds of most careers!

You can design your career in any number of ways. After all, you'll soon be your own boss! As a landscape company owner, you'll have lots of career options. You can offer general landscape services to homeowners or provide large-scale service to commercial enterprises at parks, condominium and apartment complexes, and just about any place there are plants (or should be). Whether your dream is to be a generalist or a specialist, there's a unique career awaiting you.

Low Start-up Cost

Start-up costs for getting your landscape company off the ground don't need to break the bank. In fact, many successful landscape company owners began on a shoestring budget, investing initially in a set of high-quality used tools, a mower and a reliable used truck. We'll tell you all you need to know about start-up costs later in this guide.

Often, acquiring a few residential accounts mowing lawns and performing clean-up duties where homeowners supply recycling bins is a wise first step, and will build your client base and put money in the bank. We'll tell you how to make this happen.

Unlimited Income Potential

Owning your own landscape company can become quite lucrative over time. If you are willing to learn the business inside and out, work hard, face challenges head on and persevere, your earning potential is excellent. In fact, most landscape companies charge their residential clients in the range of $25 to $50 an hour. Commercial contracts can pay significantly more. There are hundreds of landscape maintenance firms across North America that individually gross more than $500,000 annually, and plenty of room for many more.

And, the satisfaction that comes from being able to reach your full potential as an entrepreneur — creative expression, fine-tuned skills and knowledge — is often even more satisfying than the earning potential. Further good news is that 78% of respondents of *Landscape Management Magazine*'s 2008 Outlook Survey indicated that they looked forward to more work in 2008 than in 2007.

You Can Start Right Now

You don't need a college degree or a lot of start-up capital to be successful. What is the formula for success? Devoting time to learning as much as you can about the industry by studying horticulture books and trade journals; joining professional organizations and networking with other professionals; obtaining necessary licenses and certificates; becoming business savvy; and, developing trust and an excellent reputation by offering a high quality service backed by reliability and integrity.

1.2   Inside this Guide

The *FabJob Guide to Become a Landscape Company Owner* provides comprehensive and very specific information on all the important things you need to do and know to be successful in your new career.

Chapter 2 ("How to Do the Job") is an introduction to the many aspects of landscaping as a career. The chapter will start with some botany basics, and then explain the process of meeting with clients and landing a job. The chapter then covers how to plant and maintain turf, trees, and bedding plants. It concludes with a look at how you can keep busy all year.

Chapter 3 ("Develop Your Skills") will tell you how to prepare for your career before you jump right in. It explains the benefits of working for someone else for a while to learn the ropes, and then goes over formal and informal ways to boost your horticulture knowledge and career-specific skills. The end of the chapter takes a look at obtaining different certifications in this field.

Chapter 4 ("Planning Your Business") will launch you on your way to success. It covers your business options, how and why to draft a business plan, and how to determine your funding requirements. It goes over the start-up and operating expenses to expect, and where to go for financial help. The chapter ends with a round-up of legal matters from licensing to taxes.

Chapter 5 ("Managing Your Landscape Company") covers the tasks you'll need to do to run your business, such as purchasing the right equipment and tools, hiring and keeping great employees, and keeping an eye on your expenses and profit margin. It explains a number of different ways to charge your fees, and the factors to consider in setting them. Finally it takes a look at how to keep your business going for years to come by being professional on the job.

Chapter 6 ("Getting Clients") starts by explaining the difference between residential and commercial clients, and advises you what to expect from each. It then addresses the different ways you can market your services to the segments, including how to get word-of-mouth referrals to work for you. Successfully bidding on government contracts is also explained in this chapter.

The guide also contains a list of professional associations, university resources and programs, and other must-have resources to ensure success, and all the online links you'll need to get started!

Throughout the book, you'll find valuable insider advice shared by successful landscape company owners representing all facets of the industry. Find out how the owner of the largest residential landscape company in Southern California got started, and get valuable tips for success from many other owners, including the female owner of a "green-sanctioned" design/maintenance company.

Whether your goal is to grow your landscape company to dozens or even hundreds of clients and employees, or just to get out of the rat race and earn a decent living working for yourself with a handful of accounts you can manage on your own, this career guide will provide valuable insight about breaking into the industry.

Let's get started!

2. How to Do the Job

You've probably planted a lawn or garden in your lifetime, especially since you're reading this book. Landscaping for clients will follow many of the steps but may involve larger-scale projects and some newer technologies.

Most people don't put a lot of planning into landscaping their own yards — they just go ahead and do it, with mixed results. Maybe the bedding plants end up overcrowded and unattractive, or the trees become unsafe because they were planted too close to the shed and outgrow their bounds. The point of hiring a landscaper is so that no detail is missed. For this reason, we're going to break down the components of landscaping in this chapter, to turn you into the ultimate expert that your clients will brag about long after the leaves are raked up and gone.

2.1 Botany Basics

Let's talk a little bit about basic botany (plant science) and what makes a plant tick. Think of it this way. Knowing how a plant grows and functions is just as important as understanding how a lawnmower or any other piece of equipment works. Become a true expert in your field, and wow your customers with your knowledge!

2.1.1   Plants and Water

All land plants need water. In fact, about 90 percent of a typical plant is made up of water. Even desert plants with ingenious methods of holding onto water with thick succulent leaves need water to live. They're just better conservers than most other plants. Water is necessary for photosynthesis, nutrient transport and much more. Let's start with why a plant needs water and how it takes it up. Then we'll talk about what happens if it gets too much or not enough water.

The Water Cycle

Understanding where water comes from and where it goes is really pretty fascinating. In addition, applying the concept of what happens during the hydrologic (water) cycle of plants to your profession will help keep your customer's water bills down and keep their plants healthy.

Let's look at the illustration below:

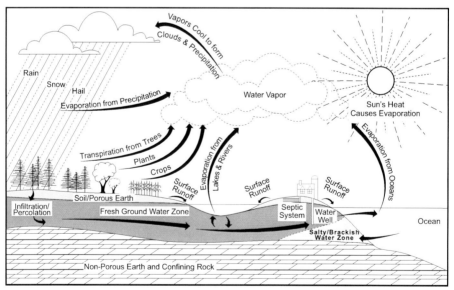

The Water Cycle. (Illustration courtesy of the Ohio Department of Natural Resources.)

Water and minerals in the soil are taken up by plant roots and move up the shoots in the xylem, which is the water-conducting system that extends from the roots to the leaves. It's a great Scrabble word, too!

How does water defy gravity like this, anyway? By an energy gradient that transports it from a higher to lower water potential. This starts with atmospheric pull causing leaf evaporation (called transpiration) and ends with water uptake by the roots.

In addition to transpiration, water is also evaporated from the soil. The combination of evaporation and transpiration is called evapotranspiration (ET). Basically, you can think of ET as the water requirements of a plant. Water used must be replaced. The driving force behind the water cycle is the sun.

> **TIP:**   Impress your clients by casually throwing this term out once in awhile, along with the Latin names of some of the landscape plants in their garden.

Okay, end of lesson. Consider yourself a budding botanist! Now that you know the basics are you thirsty for more? There are some great botany and plant biology books on the market about the workings of a plant. Some really good ones that I personally recommend are listed in Chapter 3.

Measuring Plant Water Use

Water lost through ET needs to be replaced. On a hot summer day, a single tree can lose a hundred gallons of water or more! Just like balancing your company's checkbook, ending up with not enough funds, or not enough water, to equal the demand leaves a shortfall. Since plants need water to live, you need to make sure it's available in the plant's root zone in the right amount.

If you know a ballpark ET rate for a specific kind of plant, your job is much easier. Plants are happy, your customers are happy, and water bills are lowered since lots of water is usually saved. Of course, ET varies across locations and seasonally — it's highest in summer and lowest during winter.

Fortunately, you don't need to memorize any fancy equations, get a degree in physics, or even try to measure ET yourself. That's all been done for you on enough species that we know how much water most landscape plants need. Scientists have figured out what weather factors drive ET and how to measure them. They are:

- Solar radiation

- Temperature

- Wind speed

- Relative humidity

Using this information, many states operate automated weather station networks that tell you what the ET is based on all those factors. The stations themselves kind of resemble grounded UFOs. They're strategically placed in different climates throughout the state and collect and store weather data on a minute-by-minute basis. The "Mama of All Computers," a big mainframe in a central office, calls each station and retrieves data each day and can even print out reports telling you how much to water. Pretty sophisticated!

I've incorporated everything practical that you'll need to know from these sites to run your landscaping business into this guide, but if you'd like to read more about how these weather stations work, a good example is the California Irrigation Management Information System managed by the Department of Water Resources. Visit their site at **www.cimis.water.ca.gov/cimis/welcome.jsp**.

Soil and Water

Knowing how much water a soil holds and how well it drains is very important information for you, a future landscape professional, to know. A sandy soil only holds about one-fourth as much water as a clay soil, and needs to be irrigated more often to prevent water stress. Clay soils take up water more slowly than sandy ones, too. They don't need to be watered as often but since they drain slower, they become water-logged faster.

On the other hand, if too much water is applied to a sandier soil, water may go straight through the root zone and end up inches below it before the roots have a chance to take it up. If a soil can't take up water as fast as it's applied, runoff occurs, potentially wasting large amounts of water. This often happens on a clay or compacted soil. If there's too much sodium in the water, you can end up with a big runoff problem, too. In this case, working some gypsum into the soil can help.

Here's something important to remember: a plant growing in a clay soil requires just as much water as it would in a sandy soil. But, the water needs to be applied more slowly and less often. In other words, you can go longer between irrigations but need to apply more water each time.

Rooting Depth

While you can't change a plant's genetics and plant species do vary some in their normal rooting depth, the limiting factor is usually the environment, not the genes. Sound familiar? Plants and humans are similar in that way. Most of us have enough brainpower. We just need a healthy, invigorating environment to help us reach our potential. Plants usually have decent enough genetics, too. Promoting a healthy environment lets them reach their potential.

Here's a general guideline of how deeply various kinds of plants root and how deep to water them once they're established. These depths are generalities and aren't carved in concrete, and plants vary a bit across categories, but it's a good start. Remember that limiting factors such as soil compaction or layered soils can affect the ability of the water to seep into the soil deep enough. Work the soil up well before planting, and mix in plenty of soil amendments (except at tree planting sites) to the following depths or deeper:

PLANT TYPE	DEPTH
Annual flowers	6 inches to 1 foot (15 to 30 cm)
Most shrubs Cool-season turfgrass Tomatoes	1 to 2 feet (30 to 60 cm)
Large shrubs Trees Warm-season turfgrass	2 to 5 feet (60 to 150 cm)

General Tips for Watering Landscape Plants

Here are some tips on watering landscape plants to keep them healthy and happy.

1. Hydrozone plants.

Place plants with similar water requirements together so they can be watered on the same schedule. This keeps them from being over- or under-watered.

2. Apply the right amount of water at the right time.

Base irrigations on water needs of the plant, and the soil conditions. Over-watering is more common than under-watering for both drought-resistant plants and those with higher water requirements. Many landscape trees, shrubs, groundcovers and lawns are routinely over-watered, often due to busy homeowners forgetting to reduce the amount of minutes programmed on their irrigation clock during the fall and winter when ET rates are low. Since clay soils dry out slowly, they are especially prone to over-watering.

3. Water plants deeply and infrequently.

Letting the soil dry out a little between irrigations is an excellent way of preventing root rot diseases. Watering a plant deeply encourages it to root deeper, which stabilizes it and lets it tap into a reservoir of water it couldn't reach before.

4. Water early in the morning when evaporation rates are lowest.

This can really save water since evaporation rates are low. Remind your clients that automated irrigation systems that turn on before anyone is awake need to be checked regularly for broken parts and leaks that they may never discover otherwise. Who can best do this? You or one of your crew members! Make a point of offering this service to your clients.

5. Avoid water waste below the root zone and runoff.

Sandy well-drained soils act like sieves. Water can run right through them. In fact, a lot of water is wasted this way. Plant roots don't have a chance to absorb it before it ends up below the root zone. To avoid this, apply water slowly and for shorter periods of time than you'd water clay soil. Since clay soils hold more water than sandier ones and absorb it more slowly, they are more prone to runoff than to deep percolation. To prevent runoff in heavy soils, apply water at low rates for as long as possible during each irrigation before runoff occurs.

6. Cycle water in heavy or compacted soils or on slopes.

This involves dividing the water that would normally be applied in a single irrigation into two or more shorter cycles, applied as closely together as possible when the soil is still moist. (This is different than watering every day for only a few minutes, which isn't a good practice since the water never goes deep enough.) When cycling water, it's still important to allow the soil to dry down for a few days after the necessary cycles are completed before starting the process all over again.

Water cycling can be very beneficial on slopes. It can prevent runoff at the base while supplying adequate water to the upper plantings. Although avoiding runoff completely is almost impossible, it can be greatly reduced by cycling water.

Water should be applied for 5 to 10 minutes every hour or until runoff just begins, and the cycle repeated as many times as necessary to fill the soil reservoir up again. High output sprinklers that apply water faster than it can be absorbed should be avoided; sprinkler outputs of over ½ inch (1.2 cm) per hour often lead to runoff. Drip irrigating ornamental plantings on slopes is a great way to make sure water gets into the root zone and to prevent runoff.

7. Check irrigation systems regularly for problems.

If there are brown spots in a lawn or groundcover planting not caused by insects, diseases or nematodes (microscopic worms, many of them parasites), and a "can test" (a way of evaluating how water is being applied, explained in section 2.3.1) indicates that water is not being applied evenly, problems with the irrigation hardware are likely to blame.

Common problems that you should check for include broken sprinklers, unmatched sprinklers, poorly spaced sprinklers, sunken heads, crooked sprinklers, vegetation growing around heads, and sand or debris plugging sprinklers. Correcting these problems can reduce water waste by 20 to 50 percent and greatly improve the health of the planting.

8. Add a layer of mulch.

Garden and ornamental plantings benefit from a 3 to 4 inch (7 to 10 cm) layer of mulch placed on top of the soil. Mulching is one of the most beneficial practices that you as a professional can do to keep your client's plants healthy. Mulches reduce water loss from the soil, minimize weeds, and buffer soil temperatures. While mulches are great around trees, too, they should be kept several inches away from trunks and extend outward toward the drip-line. It should not be piled around the base of a tree like a volcano!

9. Add soil amendments.

Clay soils amended with organic matter absorb a lot more water than they otherwise would. Amended sandy soils hold water longer than if they were left unamended, too, requiring less frequent irrigation.

Organic soil amendments are excellent additions to flower gardens and to soils where small woody ornamentals are desired, but should be avoided in tree planting holes. Mature trees grown in amended soil often develop circled roots that never leave the original planting hole. After all, if you were those tree roots, would you want to venture out into worse soil? All the water and nutrients are in the amended soil and that's where the roots will stay, too. Amending tree sites can lead to shallow roots and trees that topple over in the wind. It's better to put the soil that was taken out of the planting hole back in as the tree is being planted.

2.1.2   Nutrients and Fertilizers

An understanding of the nutrient needs of plants is important for maintaining healthy landscapes, and for making wise, environmentally sound management decisions.

There are 16 essential nutrients required by landscape plants, classified as either macro- or micronutrients. Micronutrients are just as important for plant growth as macronutrients, but are required in lower concentrations.

Essential macronutrients not supplied by air and water are:

- Calcium (Ca)
- Phosphorus (P)

- Magnesium (Mg)
- Potassium (K)
- Nitrogen (N)
- Sulfur (S)

Essential micronutrients are:

- Boron (B)
- Manganese (Mn)
- Chlorine (Cl)
- Molybdenum (Mo)
- Copper (Cu)
- Zinc (Zn)
- Iron (Fe)

Nitrogen is by far the most limiting nutrient required by landscape plants. Sources of nitrogen fertilizer are classified into two main categories: quickly available (fast-release) and slowly available (slow-release). As you probably guessed, the distinction refers to how soon the nutrients are available to the plant, and the length of time they remain available. Both quickly and slowly available sources of nitrogen fertilizer may be applied separately or in pre-packaged combinations containing other nutrients.

So, how do you know just what's in a bag of fertilizer? Look at the product label and learn how to crack the code. It's all there. Here's the secret: those three numbers separated by a hyphen always stand for the percentages of nitrogen, phosphorus, and potassium (always in that order) contained in the bag.

So, a bag that has "10-10-10" on the front contains ten percent nitrogen, ten percent phosphate (P_2O_5), and ten percent potash (K_2O). Add it up and you get a grand total of 30 percent nutrient content. What happened to the other 70 percent? It's a lot of carrier and some inert ingredients used as filler. That's good, though, because otherwise it would be difficult to apply the fertilizer evenly.

Sources of nitrogen that are quickly available include inorganic salts such as ammonium sulfate (20-0-0), ammonium nitrate (34-0-0), potassium nitrate, and organic forms such as urea and methylal urea. They are highly water-soluble. In the west, ammonium sulfate is often the preferred quick-release fertilizer for general use since it can neutralize high pH soils.

Many sports field and parks maintenance personnel routinely apply fast-release nitrogen products due to their low cost and convenience. It is important to remember that while fast-release fertilizers result in a more immediate response than slow-release forms of nitrogen, greater skill is needed in their application to ensure that the correct amount of nitrogen is applied and to avoid uneven spread.

No more than one pound of actual nitrogen in a quickly available source should be applied per 1,000 square feet per application. That means that a 10-pound bag of ammonium sulfate (20-0-0) contains twenty percent nitrogen (2 pounds) and will cover 2,000 square feet of turf.

> **TIP:** Applying too much fertilizer can lead to too much leaf growth, resulting in large amount of turf clippings that are difficult to grasscycle and weak, excessive growth of landscape trees.

Slowly available nitrogen products cost more than quickly available products, but last longer so you don't need to apply them as often. In many cases, they also lose less nitrogen from leaching and volatilization. Some, such as Nitroform and Hydroform, and natural organic products such as bone meal and activated sewage sludge need high temperatures and bacteria to activate, while others don't. Coated urea products slowly discharge urea through cracks in the coating. The urea enters the soil over a two or three-month period.

Slow-release products also have the advantage of not burning plants as often as fast-release fertilizers and are great for use by entry-level employees who lack experience with fertilizer applications. Uneven application isn't as risky. They are also easier to use when grasscycling, since flushes of rapid growth are easier to avoid.

Phosphorus is necessary for metabolic processes involved in plant growth and development. Deficiency symptoms show up as slow growth, stunted plants and purplish leaves. Potassium is important in water uptake and can increase drought resistance. Potassium sulfate provides sulfur in addition to potassium, and is often recommended in high pH soils to reduce alkalinity. Potassium deficiency symptoms include tip and margin burn on older leaves, and slow growth.

2.1.3   You've Got Weeds

The best definition of a weed I ever heard is: "A weed is merely a plant out of place." In other words, a beautiful native poppy growing in the middle of Dodger Stadium is probably considered a weed, as is a runner of Bermuda popping up in a flower garden. But the same poppy and grass plant carefully tended by a landscaper in someone's backyard where they're supposed to be are anything but weeds. One man's weed may truly be another man's wildflower.

The best and easiest way to cut down on weed problems is to avoid them altogether. Weeds are opportunists. They'll invade any area in the yard without something growing, and will try to out-compete landscape plants for water and nutrients. And, they're well equipped to do some damage! A typical weed produces thousands of seeds and is serious about producing another generation.

Prevent these invaders by doing everything you can to establish healthy plants quickly. If you're planting large areas of turf or groundcover, give the plants adequate water and fertilizer to create a dense planting that will shade out weeds. If your client wants you to install a desert landscape with drought-resistant plants and mulch or rocks in between, make sure you suggest to them a layer of black plastic underneath. It can really cut down on weeds seeds germinating.

So you've done all that, and in May some weeds start popping up anyway. Now what? Identify what kind of weed they are and if they're annuals (live one year) or perennials (live two or more years). A common summer annual is crabgrass. Common perennials are dandelion and Canada thistle.

Hand weeding or hoeing work best for just a few weeds. Persistent perennials in large plantings may need to be controlled with carefully applied herbicides, either before an area is planted to prevent weeds from germinating, or as a spot treatment after weeds are up. Remember that compost needs to be well decomposed before it's ready to be used. Otherwise, you might be growing a whole new crop of weeds! Finished compost smells good, and you won't be able to recognize what went into it, like twigs and grass blades. When compost is made right, weed seeds die from the high temperatures in the pile.

2.1.4   Common Plant Troubles

Proper plant selection for the intended environment is the best way for you, as a landscape professional, to ensure long-term success. After that, taking good care of plants through proper site selection, planting and maintenance practices is estimated by experts to reduce problems by at least 80%.

Just think about it. The transition for a container-grown plant from controlled nursery conditions to the landscape can be hard enough. If the plant is not properly cared for after that, there's added stress that can weaken it and make it a prime target for diseases and insects. Sometimes, even with proper care, you'll still get an occasional unhealthy plant. Some problems happen soon after planting, while others develop over time.

Likely Causes

A very common cause of plant decline and death is due to not following recommended cultural practices. This means that it's not the plant that's the problem, but how it is being taken care of. Probably the biggest mistake landscapers make once a plant is in the landscape has to do with water management. When a problem is due to uneven watering, the resulting spots can look a lot like a disease. Too little water during establishment and too much water later on kills more plants than any other factor except for poor selection for a particular climate.

Actual plant pathogens are most often not a primary cause of plant failure in the landscape. Disease development depends on a favorable climate in addition to a susceptible host. If you suspect a problem, send a sample to a plant diagnostician for help in identifying it, and study pictures on Cooperative Extension websites. (A list of these websites is provided at the end of this guide.)

Be sure you figure out what the cause of the problem is before you decide to apply any pesticides. Spraying a fungicide on an insect problem can kill beneficial microbes and won't cure the problem. In most cases, you can avoid pesticides all together just by taking good care of the plants.

A less common cause of landscape plant failure is due to insects. Sometimes the damage is hard to distinguish from a disease or a watering problem. Getting the right diagnosis is very important! To do this, you need to know what the plant is, what it should look like, and what environmental conditions it requires. Environmental stresses are very common. These occur when the weather is just too hot or too cold for a certain plant. Sometimes, it's simply due to an unusual weather pattern. Other times, it's because a plant that just can't take that particular climate was selected.

Each section in this chapter will provide more information about how to deal with common troubles of turf, trees and bedding plants respectively.

2.1.5   Environmentally Friendly Landscapes

While being a good steward of our environment has been a goal of many landscapers for decades, more and more clients across the United States and Canada are specifically requesting these services. These clients often go straight to a company promoting these environmentally friendly landscapes rather than calling what they consider a run-of-the-mill company not specifically mentioning these services in promotional materials.

In many cases, companies that have always provided services stressing principles and practices of what is now called "eco-landscaping" are changing the way they promote their business to gain a larger percentage of this growing market. Some have even changed their company's name and almost all now target this market in their advertising.

Here are practices within the field of landscaping that you can promote and orient your landscape company toward to let your prospective clients know that your company is responding in a positive, progressive way to important environmental issues.

Integrated Pest Management (IPM)

Integrated pest management emphasizes the use of prevention and sound maintenance practices to avoid disease, insect, and weed problems, and eliminate or greatly reduce the need for chemical pesticides. Incorporating these principles can greatly improve the health and vitality of a landscape, because populations of beneficial biological organisms are not reduced by unnecessary use of pesticides.

Water-Efficient Landscapes

Landscapes that use drip systems, mulches, "smart" controllers, and drought-resistant plants are a booming industry. Many landscape companies are starting to offer advice or specialize in this area.

Drought-resistant plants can be native or introduced. When customers request that only natives be planted, make sure you select only those species that do well in stressful urban environments that often have high levels of air pollution. I always suggest to landscapers that they take time to educate their clients in this area and point out that not all natives do well under modern conditions, nor are they always more drought-resistant than non-natives.

Compost Amended Landscapes

Many regions have greatly restricted how much yard and lawn clippings can be dumped in landfills. Due to this fact, there is a growing supply of compost made from recycled grass clippings and tree and shrub prunings. Compost incorporated into flowerbeds and non-tree landscape plantings can greatly improve the quality of the soil, increasing its water-holding capacity and supply of oxygen.

Energy-Efficient Landscapes

Many companies are choosing to offer hand-weeding and raking services in lieu of using power rakes and blowers to stay ahead of the growing list of cities banning these products due to noise and air pollution concerns. Those companies still using mechanical methods should be aware that manufacturers of landscape equipment are constantly offering redesigned mowers and leaf blowers that comply with the United States Environmental Protection Act (EPA) and Canada's Clean Air Act. This new equipment also has the advantage of being more reliable than older models. Even then, it is expected that the ban on leaf blowers will continue to grow throughout North America.

Sustainable Landscapes

Sustainable landscaping centers around low-input landscapes that require few resources and very low maintenance. This area is growing by leaps and bounds, and many college and universities are now offering courses and even majors in this field.

A forerunner in this movement is the University of Minnesota, which provides excellent educational materials available through their Sustainable Urban Landscape Information Series, which can be instantly accessed on their website at **www.sustland.umn.edu**. Topics include landscape design, plant selection, installation and maintenance.

A Real-Life Example: deeper greeN

Debra Amerson, proprietor of deeper greeN (**www.deepergreen.org**) in Marin County, California, is a true example of an eco-landscaper and artist who "transforms new, empty, dull and lifeless spaces into harmonious atmospheres that look beautiful, and feel warm and comfortable."

Debra's company beautifies commercial and residential spaces by incorporating tropical plants, decorative art and eclectic accessories (including Art UnderPlants self-watering systems for indoor plants, featured in the April 2005 edition of *Organic Style* magazine); deeper greeN was one of the first five businesses in Marin County to receive Green Business Certification. In order to be certified, a company must demonstrate that it has met all legal environmental requirements as well as undertaken voluntary measures to meet pollution prevention, resource conservation, and waste minimization standards.

2.2   Assessing Clients' Needs

There are three common ways a consultation meeting with a potential new client can come about. First, it can happen as a result of a follow up to a word-of-mouth agreement over the phone or email with a customer who's said they want to hire you. Often, it's the result of a referral from one of your customers. Or, sometimes you received a phone call or email from a prospective customer who's taking bids. In other instances, a neighbor or other person passing by your work site asks you to stop by their site and give them an estimate. No matter how the meeting arises, though, the steps you will follow, outlined below in this section, are the same.

2.2.1 The Initial Meeting

When you come to an initial meeting with a prospective client, it's important to arrive on time and in professional attire. Not your Sunday best, but a clean, unwrinkled company polo shirt and slacks work well. When you meet, look your customer in the eye, and offer a firm handshake. Hand them a business card, and greet them with "Hi, Mr./Mrs./Miss/Ms. _____. So nice to meet you. Let's take a walk around your property so you can show me what your needs are."

> **TIP:** If you distribute magnetized business cards, there's less of a chance they'll stick it in a drawer and lose it! Of course, you may also want to have some paper cards for other purposes.

With your clipboard in hand, jot down your customer's needs and wants, and offer thoughtful suggestions without sounding overly aggressive. Make sure you don't say something that might be interpreted as a put-down. "I like your idea of planting verbena in that flowerbed. There's a new drought-tolerant variety I can show you," sure beats, "Wow, I can see why you want to get those pansies out of there! I never did like that kind of flower." For all you know, your customer's grandchild gave them to her for her birthday a few months ago and they've just had their better day.

Don't lose a potential customer (or a faithful current one, for that matter) by being insensitive. This kind of thing happens more than you think. It's one of those things that you may never hear feedback on yourself, but neighbors on both sides of your disgruntled client as well as the whole Parent Teacher Association at the school your client's grandchild attends just might!

It's important when you meet up to really listen to your clients. Carl Clifton, founder and President of LawnScape Systems, Inc., the first lawncare company of its type in Southern California, says: "Being a good listener is one of the most important traits a successful landscape service provider needs to have. Knowing how and when to interject effectively is really important, too."

Since Carl's company now serves every major county in Southern California, provides services to more than 10,000 clients and has annual sales of more than $1.8 million, he's in a good position to offer this advice. Did I mention Carl started out mowing lawns while still in high school? What a success story.

Prepare to spend up to 30 minutes — or much more if it's an estate or commercial property — walking the site. Make sure you don't appear rushed. This is a common complaint. Don't lose a potential customer because you gave them the impression you just want to close the deal without hearing them out and thoroughly assessing the situation.

When you're finished your onsite survey, try to give them an estimate right then and there if at all possible. This will get easier over time and with experience, and you'll find more on fees and estimating work hours in section 5.4. Minimally, give them a verbal one before you leave, and schedule a follow up face-to-face meeting in a few days with the promise that you'll bring a completed contract for them to sign.

Ask if you can sit down with them and go over plans before you leave. Landscapers lose a lot of customers by appearing unenthusiastic and leaving without some firm plans for follow-up. Saying you'll mail an estimate with no given time-frame is a bad plan.

2.2.2 An Onsite Survey

Besides the specific jobs your potential customer has asked you to do (or estimate costs for), make sure you take time to do an onsite survey of everything else that needs to be included or dealt with, both related and unrelated to the work they have already brought up.

Make sure you note the location of water mains, piping, valves, heads and central controller if any of the work will involve irrigation and/or general lawncare. As you'll read a bit later in this guide, many causes of brown spots and uneven turfgrass growth can be traced back to irrigation hardware or scheduling problems.

If the work entails general fall clean up, find out how much greenwaste you'll need to either compost onsite or at another location, so you can plan your equipment and time adequately. Also, note any potentially hazardous trees and any diseased plants and/or weed problems that need to be dealt with, either by you (if you're licensed and trained in those areas) or another professional.

Talk to your potential customer about all of these issues from a positive "can do" vantage point, offering at least one solution for every problem. Sometimes it's overwhelming to a client to hear a litany of things that are "wrong" with what they considered an almost perfect landscape! Emphasize the importance of a comprehensive, coordinated approach to taking care of their landscape, even if you won't personally be doing each and every project.

2.2.3 Landscape Design

A well-designed residential landscape can be enjoyed by a family for generations. Being able to fulfill your customer's needs in a way that is compatible and complementary to the surrounding environment is crucial to the overall success of the design.

There are many design possibilities for any given area. Plants come in all sizes, forms, textures, and colors, and your biggest problem will likely be narrowing the list down rather than running out of choices. In the rare instance where there is no compatible plant for a certain location, there are numerous hardscape solutions. Upcoming sections have more resources for you to use in selecting landscaping components.

If you will be designing these landscapes yourself, make sure you listen carefully to your customer's desires. A major factor is balancing beauty with intended use and function. Ask them questions about their overall goals. Do they want privacy? Shade? An entertainment or recreation area? Plants that attract birds? Fall color?

The level of maintenance a homeowner is willing to perform (or pay you to perform) is a major factor in plant selection, too. It can make or break the long-term success of the landscape. One homeowner might dream of a backyard play area in a turf setting, while another client desires low-maintenance native plants.

Ask your customer to draw a rough plan of their initial ideas and to jot down any particular plants they have in mind. They may know exactly what plants they want, but aren't sure where to put them. Or, they may have an overall design in mind and want a major front or backyard overhaul but aren't sure what plants to chose.

In many cases, the final design for a backyard landscape incorporates the use of one or more focal-point specimen trees, along with shrubs, groundcovers, turf and garden plants. Besides planting trees based on flower color, think about including trees with interesting branching structure and bark characteristics, too. The form a majestic oak takes in January in cold climates can be breathtaking!

> **TIP:** A properly placed tree can add beauty and reduce interior energy use, which is not only good for the environment but for your customer's wallet. Illuminating the tree with well-placed lighting extends its beauty into the night, and can add an element of increased home security with a better-lit yard.

A common design mistake that beginners make is to overcomplicate a landscape, making it appear cluttered and disorganized. Often, less is more! Dynamic statements can be made with very simple designs. While varying plant shapes and forms adds interest and contrast to the overall design, remember not to overdo it.

Interspersing round, spreading plants with narrower upright types can be very appealing. So can mixing evergreen and deciduous plants (there's nothing quite like a vibrant display of fall color in New England). Just don't end up with a hodgepodge. Repeating a few effective patterns within a single theme adds unity and order and is more appealing than a random approach. For instance, planting a flowerbed with a single hue of each of several species, placed according to height and form, can dramatically improve the look and feel of the overall landscape.

When designing flower beds, also remember that adding splashes of color by planting varieties that bloom in sequence rather than all at once adds interest and gives your customers reasons to appreciate your work all summer. Group plants together in odd numbers (three, five, seven, etc.) whenever possible.

There are many excellent landscape design programs available on the Internet and in hardcopy. A few good ones (there are many out there!) that you can download free trials of and that are reasonably priced are:

- *Realtime Landscaping Pro*
  Website: **www.ideaspectrum.com**
  Phone: 1 (866) 894-4332

- *PRO Landscape*
  Website: **www.drafix.com**
  Phone: 1 (800) 231-8574

- *Master Landscape Pro*
  Phone: (816) 891-0025
  Website: **www.punchsoftware.com/products/MasterPro.htm**

- *DynaSCAPE Software, Inc.*
  Phone: 1 (800) 710-1900
  Website: **www.dynascape.com/design**

2.2.4   Timelines and Proposals

Set a Project Timeline

Drawing up a reasonable timeline is important so your customer will know what to expect during the course of the work and so you can plan your time and that of any employees who will be assigned to the project.

Make a list of everything that you and your client agree needs to be done. This should include long-term maintenance as well as shorter-term projects like planting a garden or doing some fall clean up.

It's usually easier for your client and your employees to get a quick snapshot of the scope of the work if you either sketch it out by hand lengthwise month by month on a piece of 8 ½" x 14" paper or, if at all possible, set it up "landscape style" as a computer spreadsheet.

Try to avoid using a month-by-month calendar where each month is on a different page of a multi-page document to draw up the timeline. It's difficult for your potential customer to visualize the scope of the project and keep track of the big picture when they have to flip through a lot of paper. A clear, easy-to-follow presentation of the work plan is advantageous to you and your employees as well.

List each activity and include short (but specific) descriptions and approximately how long each task will take. Make a note of which are routine and will extend over the course of the season, versus which will be accomplished during a particular season or on an as-needed basis.

Making sure the timeline is as accurate as possible based on how many hours each project will take is extremely important. Make sure you include enough people hours to conduct any pest detection activities and things like fall cleanup and soil preparation prior to planting. Don't forget to include time it will take to line up any rental equipment, subcontractors, etc. that might be necessary for certain tasks.

Presenting a Proposal

Always present a written proposal to your client, whether it's a residential or commercial project. Make sure you have included the scope of the work, all materials and supplies needed, and final costs. This is usually your final chance to persuade your potential client that your company is the right one to perform the services they're interested in receiving. Try if at all possible to meet one-on-one so you can answer any questions and address any unresolved issues.

As always, make sure to listen intently to any questions, hesitations or suggestions for changes your client has. It's much easier to discuss these things and make sure that the scope, price and details of the project are agreed upon at the outset than to make the mistake of assuming everything is alright only to find out later that there are some major misunderstandings to deal with.

Although you can't legally make changes to any formal bid, you can make changes to informal proposals you've drafted for residential work. In this case, make sure that any changes that are requested in type and amount of materials and supplies, services to be performed, or follow-up maintenance schedules are made so there's no misunderstanding.

2.2.5   Client Contracts

Once you've landed the job, it's time to prepare a final contract. It should define the scope of the work, the timeframe, all costs, and any standard warranties and legal disclaimers you and your attorney deem necessary. Regard this contract as a way to define what will be done, and a method of cutting down on misunderstandings and avoiding problems. Think of a contract as a communication tool as well as a legally binding agreement.

A contract defines the goals of the project, and how things will progress from point A to point B. It helps you schedule your time and line up any materials and supplies you'll need by a certain date. And, last but not least, it spells out the fact that there is a set period of time in which notice must be given for the contract to be canceled. Hopefully, you won't ever need to enforce this clause, but it's important it's there.

Before you ask your client to sign a contract, make sure you let them know that you value them as a customer and want to make sure the services you'll be providing are what they have in mind. It's always better to make changes before rather than after the contract is signed whenever possible.

In general, the bulk of difficult commercial contract negotiations occur between landscape contractors and clients rather than lawncare companies and clients. If you're going to become licensed and provide contractor services, expect more back and forth regarding products you'll be installing (both plants and hardscapes) from a cost and a scope perspective. Although negotiations can take some time, in a great majority of cases, workable agreements are reached. After any contract is signed, changes made (called change orders) should always be in writing.

Here are specific items that you should make sure are included in a contract. There may be others that you'll also want to include depending on the specific situation:

- Costs and quantities of plants and hardscape items to be installed

- Description of work to be done and hourly rates, including clean up

- Project start date and estimated completion date (may be month to month)

- Payment arrangements and due dates (down payment, mid-project payment and final payment)

- Plant and materials guarantee for specific time w/replacement provisions

- Legal cancellation notice (for set number of days within which contract can be voided after signing, usually three)

- Proof of required licenses/certifications you and all subcontractors hold if relevant to the project

- Proof of your insurance coverage (liability, workman's compensation, coverage of subcontractors, etc.)

On the next few pages you will find a Sample Landscape Maintenance Contract, provided courtesy of **www.Progardenbiz.com**, and reprinted with permission. Please view it as an example only. Your specific conditions may vary considerably.

2.3 Planting and Maintaining Turf

Lawns and sports fields planted with natural grass remain popular for a variety of reasons. For one thing, most people associate grass with very pleasant memories of outdoor experiences, such as lying in a soft bed of grass, running through a park barefoot, enjoying a backyard barbecue with family and friends, or hitting that first home run. I could go on and on, and I'll bet you can, too.

Besides providing a soft cushion and stable surface for football, soccer, baseball, and other sports, turf offers other benefits, too. It prevents soil loss from wind and water erosion, reduces airborne dust and glare, buffers surface temperatures, and increases soil organic matter. It also adds to the appeal of ornamental tree, shrub, and flower plantings in parks and backyards and can increase property values.

Landscape Maintenance Agreement

Name: _____

Date: _____

Address: _____

_____

_____

Phone: _____

1. The purpose of this Agreement is to set forth the terms and conditions under which Your Landscaping and Gardening Service (hereinafter called "Contractor") will provide landscape maintenance service for Customer at the above address.

2. Contractor agrees to perform the following services as outlined in the Landscape Maintenance Plans. Service under this agreement will be:

- Basic Plan   ❑ Weekly   ❑ Biweekly

- Standard Maintenance   ❑ Weekly   ❑ Biweekly

- Custom Program   ❑ Weekly   ❑ Biweekly

Service will exclude:

_____

_____

Service will include:

_____

_____

3. Contractor will furnish labor and equipment necessary to perform the above services. Customer will be charged for all material used.

4. Customer agrees to promptly notify contractor in writing of any dissatisfaction with the maintenance service to ensure that maintenance is performed as agreed.

5. Customer shall pay to Contractor at the rate of $ _____ per service call for the service herein agreed to be performed. Contractor will bill Customer and Customer shall make payment within ten days of billing date. Customer agrees to pay a service charge of $10/10 days overdue for all payments not made when due. In consideration of the extension of credit, Customer will pay a deposit of $ _____. Deposit will be applied toward final bill.

6. The terms of this Agreement shall commence on _____, 20__ and shall continue in full force and effect thereafter until it is terminated by thirty days written notice by either party to the other.

7. This Agreement shall be governed by the laws of the State of [Your State] and constitutes the entire agreement between the parties regarding its subject matter.

8. Should Contractor be required to engage the services of an attorney in connection with this agreement or to enforce payment hereunder, Contractor shall be entitled to his reasonable attorney's or collection fees.

9. Contractor guarantees that it will perform its service in a workmanlike manner. Should Customer's plantings be damaged by any failure of Contractor to fulfill its obligation under this Agreement, Contractor shall repair or replace such damaged plantings. Contractor shall not be liable for any damage due to Acts of God or Nature. Customer's right to repair and replacement are the exclusive remedies and Contractor shall not be liable for damages, whether ordinary, incidental or consequential other than as expressly set forth herein.

_____   _____
Your Signature   Date

_____   _____
Customer Signature   Date

Start Date: _____

Some areas of the country such as the Coachella Valley, which hosts more than 100 golf courses in cities like Palm Springs and Palm Desert, depend on revenue generated from the golf industry, which is no small change! More and more of these golf courses are going "eco-friendly," using recycled water for irrigation (which conserves potable water supplies) and providing habitats for birds and wildlife. In fact, currently more than 2,300 courses in the United States and Canada are members of the Audubon Cooperative Sanctuary Programs (**www.audubonintl. org/programs/acss/golf.htm**).

Keeping turf in good condition is very important. It not only looks more attractive, but well-maintained lawn and sports fields recover from wear, pest damage, and mechanical injury much better than poorly maintained ones. The popularity of outdoor sports has skyrocketed in many areas, and this overuse causes the grass to suffer from wear and tear and soil compaction. A properly maintained sports field is resilient and provides a safe surface, which increases enjoyment of the game and prevents injuries and lawsuits.

A good turf maintenance program includes proper irrigation, aeration, thatch control, fertilizing, mowing, and pest management. Let's talk about the specific aspects of these areas so you, as a landscape company owner, know where to concentrate your efforts. There are also several in-depth horticulture books that I recommend you read front to back and keep on your reference shelf. You'll find them listed in chapter 3.

2.3.1   Turf Irrigation

Thanks to modern technology, the efficiency of irrigation systems has improved a lot over the last few years. This, coupled with a better understanding of how much water turf actually needs, has taken a lot of the guesswork and waste out of watering turf.

Newly planted grass that's just starting to root needs to be watered regularly the first season. As the roots grow downward, you should water deeper but less often. This reduces disease and weed problems and strengthens the plant.

Once turf is established, water six to eight inches deep and let the soil dry out some before you water again. A good rule of thumb is to hold off on watering until the top two inches of soil have dried out. A soil probe or even a screwdriver are great tools for the job. When grass gets too dry, it's easy to tell. Your shoe print will stay there for several minutes and you'll start to notice wilt. Healthy grass with enough water won't hold a print.

Cool-season grasses such as tall fescue, annual and perennial ryegrass, bluegrass and bentgrass require about 20 percent more water than warm season grasses such as Bermuda, Zoysia and St. Augustine. Both warm and cool season grasses, like other landscape plants, tend to be over-watered rather than under-watered. Sometimes they even get too much water during the summer under high temperatures. Whoever is in charge of watering (often a homeowner) notices brown spots, and tries to correct things by cranking up the number of minutes on the controller. This is probably the biggest source of water waste in the landscape!

Problems often start when the sprinkler system isn't applying water evenly throughout the planting. Uneven watering causes some plants to get too much water while others don't get enough. Brown spots start to show up in the lawn, and rather than fix broken heads or other hardware problems, the homeowner just applies more water.

A better approach is to troubleshoot the cause of the poor uniformity. A few simple repairs and adjustments can save water, money, and frustration. Conducting a "can test" at least once a year is recommended and will determine both sprinkler output (precipitation rate) and distribution uniformity.

Doing a Can Test

Set straight-sided cans (tuna or cat food cans work great!) evenly between sprinklers. Usually about six is the minimum number to use for a typical-sized backyard. Run the sprinklers for 20 minutes, and then measure the amount of water collected.

If there's more than about a 20% difference among the amount of water collected in the cans, you can often improve the evenness of water application by doing a few simple things like straightening heads and removing weeds growing around sprinklers. Problems dealing with things like improper sprinkler head spacing, the wrong size nozzles or too much or too little pressure will take a bit more effort to fix. Some situations are tricky to diagnose, and you might want to call in a plumber or irrigation specialist.

Determine the average amount of water per can by dividing the total amount of water collected in all the cans by the number of cans. Then, multiply this number by three to give you the output per hour of the system. This is also called the precipitation rate. Once you know that, you can use irrigation scheduling guidelines based on local climates and water accordingly. You can obtain these from your local University Cooperative Extension or water district. For example, an easy-to-use California Lawn Watering Guide you can download free is available at **http://anrcatalog.ucdavis.edu/InOrder/Shop/ItemDetails. asp?ItemNo=8044**.

When using these guides, remember that grass growing in partial or full shade will use less water, and that heavy clay soils hold more water than sandier ones, but it takes longer to absorb. As mentioned, while the same amount of water is required for a lawn growing in these two soil types, the sandier soil needs to be watered more often, with less water applied since it dries out faster.

Conducting irrigation system checks is an excellent opportunity for you to shine in your customer's eyes. When you're negotiating a contract, suggest including a valuable service: conducting can tests and irrigation system checks for your customers a couple times a year. Often, the service will more than pay for itself. Keep records of how much water you've saved other clients, and show them. Tell them you'll fix and replace any broken or unmatched parts and, based on results of the can test, you'll also set up a water schedule especially suited to the needs of their plants. Offer to change their controller on a monthly basis to fit the weather pattern, too. Make sure they understand that this not only decreases water waste by 30 to 50 percent or more, but saves them money and enhances the health and appearance of the plantings.

2.3.2   Thatch and Soil Compaction

Thatch is that partially decomposed organic layer of grass roots and stems that you can see on top of the soil in a grass planting. Thatch thicker than ½ inch invites problems and should be removed. It tends to be worse on Kentucky bluegrass and Bermuda. A little thatch is good since it provides cushioning for sports play, and should be left alone. Once thatch problems start, though, they're hard to stay on top of, so get your ruler out.

You have a pair of options for thatch control. In some cases, you'll want to use both. One option is to rent a verticutter or power rake and use it gently and shallowly. If you have a heavy case of thatch, it's better to not remove it all at once. Be sure to compost what's removed and use it as a mulch or soil amendment. The other option is core aeration, which also opens up compacted soil.

For grass to thrive, it needs a strong, vigorous root system. Heavy clay soils and sports fields trounced on by players compact quickly and need to be aerated during their growing season. Sports fields, both sand and clay, usually have very compacted soil. Removing soil cores (aerating) with a rented core aerator adds oxygen and improves drainage.

Core when the grass is actively growing to help it recover from any injury. Cool-season grasses should be cored in fall or early spring and warm-season grasses in late spring or early summer. To do it right, use an aerator that removes plugs, not one with solid tines. Rent one that removes long plugs (at least two inches) that are a half-inch or more in diameter. The machine drops the removed cores onto the soil. You can leave them alone or speed up the decomposition process by dragging a piece of cyclone fencing over them. Another option is to gently break up the cores with a power rake. Mowing over the cores with a rotary mower dulls the blades and isn't such a good idea.

Keep those roots happy! They'll keep pumping water up that xylem if you do.

2.3.3   Fertilization

Nitrogen is important for green, healthy turf, especially during the season that it is most actively growing. Nitrogen-deficient turf grows slowly and doesn't fill in well. It often turns yellow and doesn't hold up well to traffic.

One or two applications of a complete fertilizer that contains nitrogen, phosphorus, and potassium is recommended annually. Five to six additional pounds of actual nitrogen per 1,000 square feet are required

Taking a Soil Sample to Determine Fertilizer Needs

It is often useful to take a soil sample from a client's landscape to determine how much fertilizer to apply based on the nutrient status of the soil and the requirements of the plant. Remember that while a lab will gladly interpret the results of the test, collecting a representative sample of soil is necessary for valid results.

Separate samples should be taken and analyzed independently if there are known differences in soil types (sandy, silt and clay combinations) across the landscape, or when different plants with varying fertilizers needs have been planted in the area previously.

Samples can be taken using a soil tube or auger, or with a spade or small shovel. Take samples in lawn areas to a depth of 6 inches, and down to one foot around tree and shrub plantings. In areas where the soil is thought to be the same, combine and mix subsamples collected randomly across the area (5-10 for small backyard areas, and at least double that for larger commercial accounts) in a clean plastic bucket.

Send a quart-sized, well-labeled plastic Ziploc bagful to a reputable soil testing laboratory after completing any required paperwork the particular lab requests. Send the sample in right away, and don't let it heat up on your truck's dashboard.

There are many very good soil testing laboratories throughout North America. A good way to find a reputable local one is through a green industry trade association referral. Prices vary according to how many analyses you need, but start at about $50-$75 for a basic test.

Always request a pH test, since the availability of many nutrients already in the soil is based on this, and don't worry about paying for a nitrogen analysis. Nitrogen is so mobile that by the time you get the results of the soil test back, the results are old news. Instead, use nitrogen fertilizer guidelines for turf and other landscape plants outlined in landscape reference materials.

throughout the growing season to maintain high quality playing fields and golf courses. Lawns and sites that aren't used so intensely only need three or four pounds over the course of a year.

> **TIP:** Grasscycling (leaving clippings on the lawn) recycles nutri-ents, reducing nitrogen requirements by 20-25%. Read more about grasscycling in section 2.3.4.

It's important to apply enough nitrogen without overdoing it. Over-fertilization can add to thatch buildup and increase mowing and water requirements by promoting too much growth. Also, nitrogen can leach below the root zone and end up polluting rivers and streams, especially in sandy soils. Because of this, it's a good idea to avoid fast-release fer-tilizers entirely in favor of slow-release nitrogen sources (sulfur-coated urea, IBDU or natural organic-based fertilizers) on fast-draining sandy soils.

Under-fertilization can present problems too, leading to weak, un-healthy grass. Lawns that don't green up after an application of nitro-gen may need other nutrients, like phosphorus or iron. A soil test will pinpoint which ones are needed and how much to apply.

Remember that soils may have too high or low of a pH to grow healthy lawns, so have that tested too (see the sidebar on the previous page), and follow recommendations from the lab. Balanced fertilizers that contain nutrients besides nitrogen, such as phosphorus, potassium, and iron, should be applied a couple times of year. The bulk of the nitrogen can be applied by itself in separate applications during the active grow-ing season.

2.3.4 Mowing the Grass

Mowing grass seems pretty straightforward. Most of you probably did it at home as kids and got the job done without really thinking much about it. But, if you're considering offering mowing as a service provid-ed by your landscape company, I want you to put on your business hat.

Think about all the benefits your company gets from maintaining the most attractive, well-tended lawn, park, or sports field in town. Your customers are happy, the grass is healthy, and it's one of the best free forms of advertising available. Think of it as a huge billboard saying, "Hire me and your lawn will look like this!"

Keeping your client's grass mowed regularly and professionally, whether it's a small backyard or an entire football field, makes a very important visual statement. In many cases, the quality of the rest of your work is judged by how good the grass looks, and mowing is a big part of the whole picture.

> **TIP:** To make this "advertising" work, always have your company's name and phone number on your trucks, and if you have one, add your website, too. More on marketing though word-of-mouth will follow in Chapter 6.

Let's talk about what happens to grass when you mow. By its nature, mowing is a destructive practice. For one thing, it reduces the leaf area available for photosynthesis. If done incorrectly, it promotes a friendly environment for diseases and weeds such as crabgrass, one of the most dreaded enemies of all. The good news is that mowing grass properly improves its density, uniformity, and pest and drought resistance. The appearance and health of thin, weak turf can be improved greatly through proper mowing.

Proper mowing involves much more than just keeping the blades on your equipment sharp (although this is very important). For healthy turf, you need to have the right equipment and mow at the recommended height on the right schedule.

The Right Equipment

There are two basic types of mowers: rotary and reel. Rotary mowers run on either electricity or gasoline. They cut grass with a high-speed, rotating blade and work well for mowing residential lawns and large sites adapted to cutting heights of one inch or higher. Reel mowers use a scissor-like action and work best on fine-textured grasses and those that prefer to be cut short (less than one inch) growing on smooth, even surfaces.

Precision and power are important. When you buy a mower, make sure it's powerful enough to do the job, maneuvers well, and is easy to adjust and maintain. Investing in a good quality machine is really important.

The Benefits of Grasscycling

There have been some big changes in how you mowed your family's lawn growing up and how lawns are mowed today. This is great news for you, your landscape company, and the environment.

For one thing, grass catchers are no longer the mainstay. Today, mowing is easier, safer, and much more environmentally sound than ever before. Many rotary mowers offer the option of recycling cut grass blades. They are called "mulching" or "grasscycling" mowers. They cut the grass into small pieces and redistribute it over the surface while you're mowing, which keeps huge amounts of greenwaste out of overflowing landfills.

Some lawn mowers that grasscycle also have a grass-catching option and are called "convertible mowers." They offer versatility by providing dual services to meet the needs of your customers, and many convert from mulch-to-bag-to-side discharge very conveniently and quickly.

How much of a difference can grasscycling really make to free up landfill space? Quite a lot! Take an example from California, with a population of 35.9 million and home to one out of every eight U.S. residents and half a million newcomers each year.

Many people moving to the Golden State want a home of their own and everything that comes with it, including some grass. Since grass clippings make up about half of the total yard waste deposited in California landfills, you can see why they're filling up so fast!

An average California lawn produces 300 to 400 pounds (146.8 to 195.7 kg) of grass clippings per 1,000 square ft (100 square meters) annually, which equates to as much as eight tons per acre (2,469 kilograms per hectare) each year.

To help turn things around, the California Integrated Waste Management Act was passed, requiring a 50 percent reduction in organic landfill deposits by the year 2000 (based on 1990 levels). The story is similar in many other parts of North America. Many states and provinces limit the amount of organic wastes in landfills and, with a national growth rate of one percent annually in the United States, this can really make a difference.

Besides helping the environment, grasscycling can benefit your business, too. On average, recycling clippings reduces the need for added nitrogen fertilizer by at least 20%. And, contrary to popular belief, grasscycling doesn't increase thatch build-up when done right.

Besides adding organic matter and nutrients back into the soil, grasscyling clippings also save lots of valuable time. Mowing isn't interrupted to empty grass catchers, which is a very labor-intensive process.

For grasscycling to work right, the turf needs to be dry and mowed regularly — at least weekly during the growing season. If it gets too tall, an option is to forego grasscycling for a while, and compost cut grass on or off site. Once you're able to resume a regular mowing schedule, you can start grasscycling again.

Other cases where bagging is preferred is on athletic fields where clippings left on the grass would interfere with play, or when the potential for a disease to spread would increase. Try to grasscycle and/or compost grass clippings for your clients whenever possible. It's good for the environment and your business.

If money is tight, buying a good used reconditioned mower equipped to do the job is preferred over spending the same amount of money on a new, but less powerful one. Don't skimp on horsepower when buying a lawnmower. Mowers with adequate horsepower last longer and stand up better to long hours of use. They get the job done faster, too, and in this business time is money.

Shop around and don't be afraid to ask questions of the right people. Many successful landscapers rely on reputable lawnmower repair shops for trusted advice on what specifications to look for in a mower and what brands last the longest.

You may wonder if this is a sound business practice for the lawnmower repair shop; after all, divulging all this information might reduce business. What usually happens is that a savvy repairman knows that being open and honest will actually increase business by instilling goodwill. They know that landscapers will return to their shop over and over to have blades replaced and sharpened.

There are many honest and knowledgeable equipment dealers out there, too, and visiting landscape tradeshows (see section 5.1 on purchasing equipment for more information) is a great way to mingle with them and check out the latest equipment. Most shows are free or very inexpensive; after all, they want your business!

One landscaper we interviewed offered this advice: check out equipment specifications from reputable companies online or in hardcover catalogs, then quietly hang around trade show manufacturer/dealer booths that offer the equipment you're considering buying. By doing this, you can check out lots of equipment at one place and also get a firsthand account of how many satisfied and not-so-satisfied customers each dealer has.

"It takes a pretty brave salesman to stand around his booth all day if he knows he's going to be bombarded with a bunch of ticked-off customers looking to hunt him down. Usually you find pretty honest people working tradeshows, especially if their company's been around for a long time," he explains. He's got a point.

You're also going to want to make sure the mowers you choose have easily adjustable cutting height capabilities. Traditionally, you adjust a mower by raising or lowering the wheels or by pushing and releasing a lever. Many mowers now feature tool-free deck height adjustments. Be sure to read the owner's manual carefully to stay safe and prolong the life of the mower!

Mower blades need to be sharpened regularly to maintain both the aesthetic appeal and the disease-resistance of the grass. A clean cut also decreases damage to the grass. With a rotary mower, blades should be sharpened several times a season. You can do it yourself or have a specialist at a mower repair shop do it for you, which is often the best idea.

Sometimes replacing a blade is easier and less expensive than continuing to sharpen old rotary ones. An experienced professional can often give you some very good advice about which way to go. Reel mowers require special sharpening equipment and should be taken in for service regularly.

Mowing Height

A common mistake made by both professionals and homeowners is cutting grass too short. All plants need adequate leaf area to produce food (a major result of photosynthesis) and mowing turf too low starves it, resulting in a thin, weak stand. Lawns and sports fields maintained at the right height are also better able to compete against weeds, and are more drought-resistant than grass kept too short.

Setting the cutting height too low also increases the risks of "scalping" the grass, which not only looks bad but is unhealthy. Scalped lawns resemble a bad haircut and often occur on uneven terrain and under conditions of heavy thatch. Scalped turf removes living tissue, exposing plant crowns, dead leaves, and bare soil.

> **TIP:** Some landscapers mow the grass slightly shorter than usual to remove dead grass and debris the first mowing of the season. In this case, scalping is more likely, so be extra careful.

The following table lists a range of recommended mowing heights for different species of turfgrass. When each species is healthy and actively growing, mow it nearer the lower end but raise the height when the grass is under stress from high temperatures, drought, or insects or diseases.

How often should you mow? Gauge how often you mow by how fast the grass grows. The growth rate will change throughout the season and is influenced by many things besides the weather, such as the grass species and how much fertilizer and water have been applied.

Turf Species	Mowing Height
Fine-leaf fescues	2 to 3 in. (5 to 7.5 cm)
Tall fescue	2 to 3 in. (5 to 7.5 cm)
Perennial ryegrass	2 to 3 in. (5 to 7.5 cm)
Kentucky bluegrass	2 to 3 in. (5 to 7.5 cm)
Creeping bentgrass	¼ to ¾ in. (½ to 2 cm)
Zoysiagrass	1 to 1.5 in. (2.5 to 3.8 cm)
Buffalograss	2 to 3 in. (5 to 7.5 cm)

The key is to mow based on the growth rate of the grass, rather than on a strict day-of-the-week schedule, removing no more than one-third of the length of the grass blade each time you mow. The "1/3 rule" promotes healthy roots and drought resistance.

Unless you're mowing athletic fields and specifically want a striping effect, it's also a good idea to change directions each time you mow. (Golfers particularly don't like the roll of their ball influenced by whoever mowed last!) Alternating the direction of the cut allows the grass to grow upright and reduces wear and tear in the same spot. Overlap your cutting path by a few inches each swath that is mowed and cut it when it's dry to keeps the mower from clogging. In shady areas, keep the grass slightly taller than is usually recommended to improve light absorption.

2.3.5   Common Turf Problems

Doing whatever it takes to keep turf healthy is by far the best protection against diseases, insects and weeds. Watering, fertilizing, and mowing correctly, as well as keeping the soil well drained and thatch levels down prevents at least 80% of turf diseases. Stressed grass is much more prone to outbreaks than healthy grass. Potential for disease and pathogens is almost always present in the turf environment. The key to remember is that infection won't occur without the right environment (temperature, water, light, etc.). That's why taking good care of the grass is your best bet to avoid diseases.

It all starts with planting the right grass. Make sure you choose one that not only grows well in your climate but also is going to be able to stand up to intended use. Some, just by their nature, take more wear and tear. It's important to identify problems early. This means staying on top of things and walking the site often enough (usually once a week) to catch anything right away. The longer a problem goes unnoticed, the worse it often becomes. And, once the grass is hit with one thing, it becomes weak and more likely to contract something else. In that way, plants are a lot like you and me. When we have a cold, even though it's tempting to ignore it and just keep going full speed ahead, it usually backfires and we're down longer than had we taken care of ourselves.

Turf Diseases

It's important to identify the potential disease before you try to control it, especially if you're thinking about spraying it with a pesticide. Some common diseases make the grass look bad for a few weeks but don't cause any long-term problems once the weather sides with the grass again. Spraying a fungicide on what turns out to be a watering or insect problem doesn't cure the problem and actually hurts the turf by killing off the "good guy" microorganisms. Few, if any, fungicide applications should be necessary if you choose your grass right and take good care of it.

Damage that looks like it's from a disease is often caused by incorrect watering. In fact, this is the most common mistake made. Brown spots from uneven watering cause lots of confusion. That's where those can tests and walk-throughs come in that we talked about earlier.

Other causes may be uneven fertilizing, scalping from mowing too low, lawn chemicals or insects. Or, it could be a problem due to the weather. Maybe it's hotter or colder than normal. If you do have a lawn disease, it's probably caused by a fungus. You might see spots on the leaves, or yellow or thin grass, rotted roots, or small or large circles with a "frog eye" (healthy grass in the center of dead grass).

For help identifying diseases, submit a sample (as described earlier) to a reputable lab. It may also be useful to look at pictures on websites for

Taking a Soil Test to Identify Turf Disease

When you're pretty sure there's a disease outbreak, it's a good idea to get a professional involved. In this case, you'll want help from a plant pathologist, a scientist who studies plant diseases. You don't need to always have a specialist visit the site (which can be expensive and wastes valuable time if no one can come out right away) each time.

You can take your own sample and send it to a reputable lab. Learning how to take a good sample is important since an accurate diagnosis depends on it. Do this as early in the game as possible.

To take a sample, collect entire grass plants (including leaves, stems, and roots) along with at least three inches of soil, from several areas. You don't have to use a fancy expensive soil sampler. A small shovel or hoe works just fine. Make sure you sample the edge of the infection, including some healthy and some unhealthy tissue in the same sample. Sending in a bunch of dead grass won't help much. All the lab will end up telling is that you've got dead grass.

Put the samples in a plastic bag and label it. Wrapping the sample in moist paper towel helps keep the samples from drying out. Attach a written description of the type of lawn and symptoms. Also, include information on the history of the site and how you've been taking care of the grass. Keep the samples dry and moist (the dash of your truck in 100 degree weather isn't the place!) and mail them in or drop them off right away.

There are many sources for locating a credible soil testing laboratory. A good online source with explanations of services offered can be found on the National Sustainable Agriculture Information Service website at **http://attra.ncat.org/attra-pub/soil-lab.html**.

Prices for soil testing vary depending on how many analyses are needed and how many samples you submit, but generally range from $50 and up.

photographs and descriptions of several common lawn diseases, such as the following. Also, Cooperative Extension contacts for each state are listed at the end of this guide. Most offer specific information on turf and lawn diseases.

- *University of Florida*
  http://edis.ifas.ufl.edu/TOPIC_Turfgrass_IPM

- *North Carolina State University*
  www.ces.ncsu.edu/depts/ent/clinic/

- *University of California*
  http://www.cals.ncsu.edu/plantpath/extension/clinic/

Insects

Insects are usually not a serious problem on turf, especially when the right grass is chosen and is well cared for. This means watering, fertilizing, dethatching, mowing, and aerating correctly. Grass that is healthy stands up better to insect attack than stressed grass.

All that said, your clients may still get some insect damage. It usually shows up as small, scattered patches of yellow or brown lawn. Diseases, lawn chemicals and even dog urine can look very similar so make sure you know what you're looking at. If you do see a bug or two, don't overreact. Many insects you'll uncover are "good guys" and are winning the war against the "bad guys."

Common beneficial insects include predatory ants, ground beetles, and ladybird beetles. That's why spraying before you find out what's actually causing the problem isn't a good idea. And, even one or two "bad" insects don't usually need to be killed with an arsenal of chemicals, especially if you don't see any turf damage. Many don't do much harm in small numbers; only one or two per square yard aren't going to hurt the grass as much as you might end up hurting it by wiping out predators.

Know what levels of specific insects are acceptable before you spray. There are some great sites online that discuss what these levels are. They vary by area, so check your local Cooperative Extension publication website listed at the end of the guide. If you find a species of insect in levels greater than their threshold, you should think about trying a non-chemical product such as *Bacillus thuringiensis* or beneficial nematodes (the good guys!) before jumping right into a chemical control. If you do decide to use a chemical insecticide, follow the label directions carefully.

Insects that may cause damage include root and leaf-feeding caterpillars such as white grubs (the larvae of beetles), masked chafers, billbugs, and chinch bugs. Each insect leaves its own clue to its identify. Some of these culprits can be seen just by looking at the grass with the naked eye or with a 10X hand lens. Other are smaller, nocturnal, or just trickier and you need to outsmart them in order to even find them.

A drench test is a great way to bring adult and larval insects that feed below the soil up to the surface so you can tell how many there are. It works great on insects other than white grubs and billbug, which you can sample for by digging. Mix two or three tablespoons of liquid dish soap into a watering can containing two gallons of water. Evenly pour the solution over one square yard where you see symptoms. If you have lots of insects, some will start surfacing right away. Wait ten minutes to make sure that even the slowpokes get counted. If none come up, it could be because the insects causing the damage are no longer active, or that insects aren't the cause of the problem.

Plant-Parasitic Nematodes

These are not the same "good guys" sometimes used for insect control. While both are tiny roundworms and are 1/50 to 1/16 inch (0.4 - 1.5 mm) long, the ones that injure turf feed on the plant, whereas the beneficial nematodes don't. In Florida and California, root-knot nematodes can damage and even kill turf. Nematodes attack all species of grass and leave patches of yellow, wilted plants. Irrigating, fertilizing and aerating correctly can prevent damage.

Root-knot nematodes cause galls to form on roots that can lead to disease outbreaks. Sodded lawns growing in sandy soils can have major nematode problems. The only way to really know if your client has a nematode problem is to send a soil/root sample to a reputable lab.

Try to prevent nematodes from becoming a problem; it's almost impossible to get rid of a bad case. Prevention is key.

Weeds

As mentioned earlier, the best and easiest way to prevent a huge weed problem in your client's lawn is to avoid them altogether. They'll take over thin areas pretty quickly, so make sure the grass is healthy and thick and establish a new lawn quickly. This will not only keep weed seeds from germinating, but helps the grass out-compete any weeds that do sneak in. Remember that weeds produce thousands of seeds, so prevention is key. Following recommended irrigation, fertilization, mowing and aeration practices will really help the grass stay ahead of the game.

With all this said, you'll probably still get a weed or two. Know what it is. There are several free online sources to help you identify common weeds growing in turf. Click on the Cooperative Extension publication site for your location (listed at the end of this guide) for specific help, and search for "turf weeds" or "lawn weeds."

Other helpful sites include:

- *Michigan State University's online pictorial guide*
  Includes most of the peskier Midwestern weeds
  www.msuturfweeds.net

- *Home Lawn Weed Control*
  For weeds in Missouri and the lower Midwest states
  http://extension.missouri.edu/explore/agguides/hort/ g06750.htm

- *Weed Photo Gallery (University of California)*
  Weeds of the Southwest
  www.ipm.ucdavis.edu/PMG/weeds_common.html

In most cases, hand weeding or light hoeing is all you'll need to do if you're maintaining a client's lawn. Larger plantings with more serious problems may require chemical control. Get to know some reliable licensed pest control advisors/applicators that you respect and trust. Recommend their services to your customers, or consider getting a state license yourself (see section 4.4.3 on licensing).

2.4 Planting and Maintaining Trees

Trees are considered by many people to be the most important part of their landscape. They add beauty, provide shade, and even help clean the air and lower energy bills. Making sure their trees are well cared for is very important to homeowners, and often they turn to their landscaper for help. Being prepared with answers raises their respect for you and protects their investment.

As a landscaper, your job may include planting and providing general care for trees. Here are some things you should know.

2.4.1 Tree Selection

Tree selection is really important. A tree is a long-term investment and should be carefully chosen. Get to know local nursery professionals that you can count on to carry high-quality trees. The health and quality of a tree also depends on a good site match, so learn what species do best in your area.

Once you've helped your client decide on a kind of tree and where to plant it, offer to pick it out, deliver it, and plant it for them for a fair profit. Many homeowners don't have the space in their personal vehicles to transport a large tree themselves, and really appreciate this professional service. Here are some more tips on this topic.

Assessing the Client's Space

When a client tells you they want to plant a tree, walk around the yard with them and talk to them about microclimate conditions, like shade and wind. Let them know how important it is to select a tree based on its ultimate size at maturity, rather than how cute it looks when it's young. Really emphasize this.

Sometimes a specific location just isn't compatible with the needs of a tree. It's better to point this out to your customers ahead of time rather than after it's too late. A tree that is going to grow 50 or 100 feet tall does a lot better in a park or a large open backyard than under power lines or next to a house. Topping it to try to make it fit damages the tree and the tree itself becomes a hazard, sometimes dropping large limbs or toppling altogether.

Instead, if space is limited, help your customer choose a tree that won't grow more than 25 feet tall, or an attractive shrub or piece of hardware. And remind them that large trees should not be planted less than 25 feet from houses and other structures. Urban trees need special care. After all, they're away from their natural environments and a lot can go wrong!

In addition to the aboveground needs of a tree, what goes on underground is just as important. It's very common for people to forget about roots and their requirements since they're hidden from view. Tree roots need lots of space to grow and they're not the best friends of sidewalks, driveways and structures.

They also need good drainage and deep soil. Drainage is especially important. You should check it before you decide to plant a tree in a particular place. Here's a simple way to do it. Dig a 30″ hole and fill it with water. Wait 24 hours and fill it up again. If the water level drops two inches or more in two more hours, drainage is good. If you find out there's a drainage problem, you should rethink planting a tree there.

Selecting the Right Tree

Before you recommend a particular tree, ask your client what their goals are. Do they want to grow their own fruit? Do they want shade? Maybe they are bird-lovers and want to attract songbirds. Or maybe they just want some privacy.

When customers have their hearts set on a specific kind of tree but their choice of locations isn't a good match, see if there's a better place to plant the tree they want before you give up. Also, make sure you have a couple alternative species in mind if case their first choice isn't available or is not in as good condition as it should be.

Fortunately, there are many tree species to choose from in any given climate, for all kinds of uses. Evergreens stay green all year, and deciduous trees drop leaves in the fall. Both may be native or introduced species and offer long-lasting beauty.

Variety is the spice of life. This holds true for trees just as much as anything else. In fact, planting several species can reduce disease and insect problems and add beauty and diversity to the landscape. Look at what happened to thousands of American Elms in the Midwest in the '70s. Many died from Dutch Elm disease and areas heavily planted to that single species were hit hard.

Tree Selection Resources

On your quest for the perfect tree for your client, become familiar with recommended Internet websites listed in the Resources section of this book. Many have excellent pictures of trees at different growth stages.

Other good resources are city foresters or arborists and local University Cooperative Extension offices. And, don't forget the local arboretum or botanical garden where the trees are labeled, making it easy to identify them.

The International Society of Arboriculture publishes a series of brochures on quality tree care as part of its Consumer Information Program called Trees are Good. Examples include Tree Selection, Proper Mulching Techniques, Avoiding Tree Damage During Construction, and Mature Tree Care. You can find them at **www.treesaregood.com**.

The National Arbor Day Foundation publishes a series of Tree City USA Bulletins on a variety of tree care topics, including: Don't Top Trees, How to Hire an Arborist, Plant the Right Tree in the Right Place, How to Prune Young Trees, and many more. They are available at **www.arborday.org**.

A real staple that you should have two copies of (in your truck and on your desk!) is a regional Sunset Garden Book. These books include more specific climate zones than the United States Department of Agriculture zones, and are true goldmines of information. You can look up trees by either common or scientific name and find out everything you need to know about their size, flower color, bloom period, unique qualities, and suitable zones. You can find them at **www.oxmoorhouse.com/ category/garden/regional+gardening.do**.

Once you get to the nursery, you'll find trees in containers, bare-root, and/or balled and burlapped (called B&B in the industry). In the West, trees are often sold in containers, while colder climates offer more B&B and bare-root stock (deciduous trees only).

Each type has its pros and cons. Bare-root trees are my favorite because the root system isn't in soil, so roots don't have to grow through one soil into another once the tree is planted. They also tend to be less expensive and are not as heavy to handle, but you have to be careful to keep the roots moist.

If you go with a container tree, be careful to check out the root system first. Gently remove the tree from the container; a healthy plant has about 50 percent roots and 50 percent soil showing around the edge.

Watch out for more roots than soil, and circled and kinked roots. Sometimes the top growth of these trees looks great and the tree may be larger than others, and may even be on sale. Red light! Stay clear of the temptation to buy one of these. It will likely show signs of decline in a few years and may even die. The problems that are already showing up will only get worse over time. Also, choose trees with well-spaced branches and trunks that don't have damage.

Trees can be just fine in the nursery but get hurt during the trip home. Protect the buds and leaves from wind by wrapping or covering them as well as any branches that might rub against your truck. Gently secure the tree in one place and drive slowly.

2.4.2   Planting Trees

Plant your client's tree as soon as possible, especially if it's bare-root. If you can't plant it for more than three days, have the nursery store it for you. If it's only a couple days, you can store it yourself on the north side of a building away from direct sun and heat. Make sure to keep the roots moist.

It's a good idea to have the planting hole dug ahead of time. Trees like well-drained soil rather than compacted, hard soil that they have to fight their way through. While adding soil amendments to landscape soil works great with other plants, they're not compatible with tree planting sites and shouldn't be used.

Why? A tree transplanted into amended soil has it made and knows it! The soil is usually much better quality than what's around it. So the tree has no incentive to venture out into the not-so-great unamended landscape soil a few feet out.

What happens? You guessed it. The roots grow in circles, just like they do in a too-tight container. It's better to just use the original soil. An exception is a very heavy clay soil; it may benefit from some added compost mixed deeply and evenly into the native soil in a very wide planting hole.

When you plant, dig the hole as wide as possible — at least twice the width of the container, but no deeper. The wider the hole the better. Trees grown in containers may need to have their roots straightened a little before planting.

Plant trees at the same depth they were in the container or slightly higher. Planting them too deep can lead to lots of problems. Remove soil from the planting hole, break it up, and etch the inside contour of the planting hole with a shovel to break up the soil. This encourages root growth. Then fill the hole half full with the same soil, lightly tamping it to remove air pockets.

Place the tree upright in the hole and water it in slowly before filling up the rest of the hole with the remaining soil. Water again, gently and slowly. Keep the roots of bare-root trees moist while they're waiting to be planted. Dig the hole and mound some soil in the center. Put the roots on top of it and let the roots cascade downward. The root flare should be at soil level.

B&B trees need to have their root ball supported with your hands as you plant them. Be careful not to drop the tree into the hole and keep the root ball intact. The root flare and top of the soil ball indicate the original planting depth.

Remove all twine and the burlap as far down as possible. Sometimes the root ball is wrapped with non-degradable fabric; be sure to remove it. If the root ball is supported by a wire basket, bend it below the soil surface and remove the wire once the tree is in the hole.

See the next page for illustrations that demonstrate proper planting techniques.

Proper Planting Technique —
Container Tree

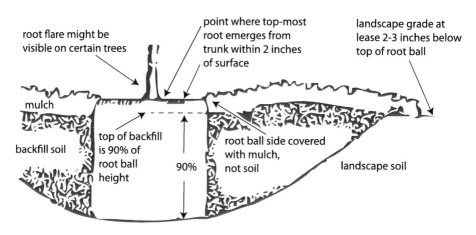

An example of the proper technique to plant a container tree.
(Illustration courtesy of Dr. Edward Gilman, University of Florida.)

Proper Planting Technique —
Balled and Burlapped Tree

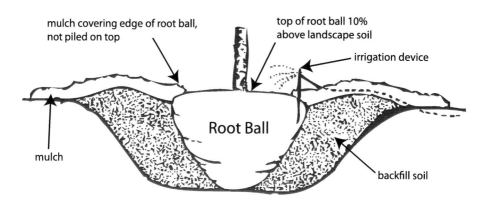

An example of the proper technique to plant a balled and burlapped tree.
(Illustration courtesy of Dr. Edward Gilman, University of Florida.)

Staking and Pruning

If trees were never staked in the nursery, in most cases you wouldn't have to stake them in the landscape. But, the reality is that they are usually tightly staked when you buy them and have been for some time. If you remove the stakes and tape, the trees will probably fall over, since the base of the tree never had a chance to strengthen. The best option in this case is to restake the tree loosely, allowing it to blow gently in the wind but not fall over.

Stakes should be driven into the sides of the planting hole before you backfill to protect the root ball. Use straps or hose to secure the tree to the stakes; don't use wire because it will cut into the bark of the tree. Over time (within about a year), you may be able to remove the stakes entirely. Of course, trees planted in really windy areas may need permanent staking. Even then, they should never be staked rigidly; a couple inches of "give" is important. In less windy areas, you can use temporary wind barriers made out of plastic or cloth for a year or so to give the tree a chance to develop a strong root system.

Unpruned trees establish faster and develop stronger root systems than those pruned at the time of planting. Sometimes minor corrective pruning is needed, though, like removing broken and damaged branches. Do the majority of pruning and training in a few years.

Watering and Fertilizing

Newly planted trees, like all plants, need to be kept moist until they're established. This is usually a whole growing season. A good way to water a newly planted tree is to make a berm around the tree and fill it with water. Or, water it using a small stream of water from a garden hose until roots are thoroughly soaked. As trees mature, the watering schedule should change, with deeper and less frequent watering. Keep trunks dry!

Newly planted trees also don't need to be fertilized right away, but many landscapers add a balanced slow-release fertilizer in the planting hole. If you decide to fertilize, don't use a fast-release form of nitrogen, which may burn the tree.

2.4.3   Ongoing Maintenance

Trees need lots of care the first few years. Nurturing them while they're still young really pays off in the long run.

Watering

Maturing trees should be watered more and more deeply, and less often over time. The type of soil they're growing in has a lot to do with how often they should be watered. Clay soil holds more water than sandy ones, so trees growing in heavy clay soils need to be watered longer than those growing in sandier soils, but not as often.

Although trees vary in how much water they need, in general, mature trees do well on about 10 gallons of water per inch of trunk diameter during each watering during the summer. When possible, water trees separately from surrounding plants. Grass and other plants can rob trees of water, and should be kept several inches away.

Trees don't need nearly as much water in winter as summer, but do need some. Before you water, check the soil moisture three to six inches deep. If it's dry or nearly so, water. In dry climates, drip systems work great because they slowly apply water into the root zone. Relying on lawn sprinklers to adequately water trees isn't a good idea, since trunks often get wet, and trees get watered too often. Reradiated heat from buildings and streets increases water demand. For this reason, trees in large open landscaped areas and parks often require less water than those on the south or west sides of a house.

Remember that roots grow outward from a tree a long way (2-3 times beyond where the foliage ends), even with deep water. Be sure to water a little further outward each season to keep growing roots moist.

Mulching

Landscape trees benefit from organic mulches applied on the top of the soil. Large-screened compost and wood and bark chips make great mulches and keep organic matter out of landfills.

Add a three- to four-inch (7.5 to 10 cm) layer several feet out from the base of the tree, keeping it at least a foot away from the trunk. Mulch holds soil moisture, reduces weed problems, and prevents what I call lawnmower and weed-eater blight! Mechanical damage can really hurt a tree. You might even want to apply a landscape fabric under the mulch as a second weed barrier.

Fertilizing

It's often beneficial to apply moderate amounts of slow-release nitrogen fertilizer to the soil over the root zone of young trees. Too much is bad for the tree and can end up polluting groundwater.

A general recommendation is to evenly broadcast a complete fertilizer (e.g., 15-15-15 or 11-4-8) at the recommended label rate (usually one-third to one-half pound of actual nitrogen per inch of trunk diameter) over the soil surface to the drip line of the tree — or even slightly beyond — to encourage their growth.

Mature landscape trees generally do not need regular fertilization. They may benefit from applications at half the rates listed for young trees, applied in spring prior to rapid growth and again in mid-summer.

Fertilizers should always be watered in well. Too much nitrogen produces flushes in growth, increasing the water requirement, and salts in fertilizers may burn roots when there isn't enough water. As trees mature, look for symptoms of nitrogen deficiency (yellow older leaves), and only fertilize if you really need too. Very old trees usually don't need to be fertilized at all.

Diseases and Insects

As always, prevention is the best approach. You shouldn't have to routinely apply pesticides if you're taking good care of the tree. And, by now you know how to properly select, plant, and maintain trees, which go further than anything else to prevent pest problems from occurring in the first place.

One of the most important preventive measures you can take is to keep trunks dry. If you notice a problem, have it identified right away. Even if you have a disease, it may not need to be treated with a fungicide. Many are not serious and take care of themselves over time.

2.4.4   Pruning Trees

Good pruning removes structurally weak branches while maintaining the natural form of the tree. Pruning is done to remove dead or hazardous branches, improve the tree structure, and to increase light and air movement. Properly pruning young trees is important for long term health and stability. Providing a solid framework improves structural stability, increase the life of the tree, and saves money in the long run. A well-trained tree develops a strong structure that requires less corrective pruning as it matures.

It's important to know that trees do not "heal" the way people do. When a tree is wounded (which happens every time it's pruned) it needs to form a callous around the cut. A small cut does less damage to the tree than a large cut. Waiting to prune a tree until it is mature can create the need for large cuts, which should be avoided.

Trees should always be pruned according to standard professional guidelines. The ISA (**www.isa-arbor.com**) and American Society of Consulting Arborists (**www.asca-consultants.org**) websites include specifics on these standards.

Trees should never be topped. Instead of pruning a tree for clearance, choose trees based on their ultimate size in the first place. Topping trees (giving them that crew-cut look!) is harmful and can result in injuries and lawsuits. Trees should always be pruned to conform to their natural shape. A well-pruned tree doesn't look like much has been done to it.

How and When to Prune

Routine pruning to remove deadwood can be done at any time. Generally, it is easiest to prune live wood when it is dormant. Flowering trees should generally be pruned after they bloom, although there are exceptions. Check with your local chapter of the ISA and your local Cooperative Extension office for specific recommendations in your area.

> **TIP:** Special care needs to be taken to not spread diseases, so avoid pruning infected trees during vulnerable states.

A major goal of "training" (selecting a central leader and doing necessary structural pruning and thinning early on) young trees is to establish a strong trunk with sturdy, properly spaced branches. The strength of the branch structure depends on the relative size of the branches, the branch angles, and the spacing of the limbs.

These vary by tree species. Some trees, such as pin oaks and liquidambar, have upright shapes with strong central leaders. Others, like elms and live oaks, are broader-spreading and don't have a central leader. Still others, such as ornamental figs and Bradford pears, are more densely branched.

Usually, a single leader should be allowed to develop. Select the strongest, most upright leader, and remove the others. Temporary, lateral branches should be left in place for a few years. They help ensure a sturdy, well-tapered trunk that's protected from the sun and mechanical damage. They should be kept short enough to avoid competition from permanent branches.

Leaving lower branches on a tree helps it develop a strong structure as it ages. Preferably, half of the branches should be in the lower 2/3 of the tree. It is sometimes challenging to follow this rule for street trees, which need at least 16 feet of clearance for traffic, but it can be done. Trees used as screens or windbreaks are much easier to train like this.

Good Quality   Poor Quality

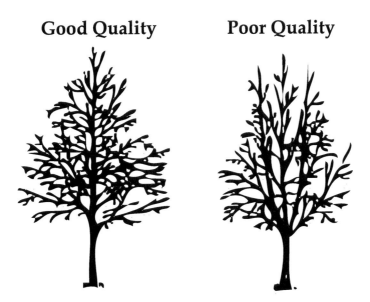

Branch structure of a good quality tree and a poor quality tree.
(Illustration courtesy of Dr. Edward Gilman, University of Florida.)

Another important aspect of pruning young trees is developing the right branch arrangement along the trunk. In general, permanent branches should be spaced about 18 inches apart for a tree expected to reach 50 feet, or about seven inches apart for a tree reaching 20 feet. These branches should also be well spaced around the tree. You don't want to end up with two branches next to each other on the same side of the tree.

Many trees, by nature, have branches with narrow angles of attachment to the main trunk. These branches should be pruned while the tree is still young. Otherwise, over time, bark can become embedded in the crotch leading to branch failure later on. And, don't use wound dressings. Research over the past 20 years has shown that they do not benefit a tree.

Proper tree pruning requires the right tools. Never use hedge shears to prune a tree! For small trees, most of the cuts can be made with hand pruning shears (secateurs). The scissor type or bypass blade hand pruners work better than anvil shears because they make cleaner, more targeted cuts. Pruning cuts larger than one half-inch in diameter should be made with lopping shears or a pruning saw. Tools need to be cleaned and sharpened regularly.

Always make cuts just outside the branch collar rather than flush cut. Mature limbs can literally weigh a ton! They should be undercut 12"-18" from the point of attachment with a second cut a few inches further out the limb. Then, cut the stub back to the branch collar.

Pruning Mature Trees

Older trees can't close pruning wounds as well as younger trees. If the trees were trained well when young, they'll only need to have dead or hazardous limbs removed and possibly some light thinning. In general, less than one-fourth of the leaf-bearing crown should be removed during any given pruning. Too much routine thinning can zap stored energy reserves causing poor health and stressed trees.

It is wise to link up with a Certified Arborist to assess and prune trees taller than those you can prune from the ground. He or she is a specialist in tree care. Make sure any arborist you contract out or recommend for hire is not only bonded, licensed, insured, and registered with the state (required in some cases) but also professional, reputable and knowledgeable. Ask for and talk to references and look at the actual work. Find out if they are active members of organizations such as the ISA, mentioned earlier in this guide. Avoid anyone who tops trees at all costs!

If You Want to Become an Arborist...

If you decide that becoming an arborist is a career you want to pursue yourself, take steps to train for and pass required exams. Usually, you'll need a couple years of actual field experience before you're eligible to move forward.

Sharon Lilly, the educational director of the ISA, got her career start in high school working for a neighbor who owned a tree service. She's been an arborist ever since, attaining international status.

Although she has a college degree, she learned the ropes and fell in love with the profession while still a teenager. When asked what the big draw is, she says, "Pruning trees is great. You get to be outside and there is immediate satisfaction from being able to see the results of your work right away, rather than having to wait several days to see a lawn green up from fertilization."

2.4.5   Damage and Hazards

Now that your client is well on his or her way to growing a beautiful, healthy tree thanks to your help, watch out for activities that can cause harm later. These include lawn renovation, underground utility and irrigation system installation, and construction of sidewalks, driveways, patios, or room additions. Tree roots don't like to be buried or have their roots cut into. Here are common mistakes you should avoid. Doing so will allow your client to enjoy their tree for many years.

- Trenching through the root zone. Tree roots need protection from construction activities. Installing cable television wires or other underground utilities, sidewalk repair, curb construction, and other similar activities can have negative impacts on the root system.

- Paving too much of the tree's dripline. Tree roots grow outward two to three times beyond the dripline of the tree. Tree roots need oxygen and water, and pavement in this area reduces both.

- Changing the grade. Changing the grade around a tree compacts the soil and buries tree roots. If a lawn or landscaped area is being regraded, make sure the excess soil isn't piled around the tree.

How to Recognize a Hazard

As a landscaper, you will probably run into lots of cases where you "inherit" tree problems that you aren't the cause of. You'll likely see your share of unhealthy trees, since they live so long and have had more time to be injured than other landscape plants.

The causes of unsafe trees include human error, diseases and insects, and weather. In a lot of cases, poor root growth, poor tree structure due to topping, and overall decline due to construction damage are to blame.

TIP: Mushrooms growing around the base of trees may indicate heart rot. Call a professional arborist if you see this.

Falling tree branches can weigh a few tons and can cause a lot of damage to buildings and cars in the area. Worse yet, they can severely injure and kill people. Sometimes entire trees topple. Always be on the lookout for trees that present a danger to your client or their property. Call in a professional arborist if anything looks suspicious.

2.5 Planting and Maintaining Bedding Plants

Flowers planted in beds, called bedding plants, add color and interest to a landscape. The sky's the limit on how bold a statement you can make with well-placed bedding plants. You can add a splash of vibrant color to make a specific area really stand out, or create a serene, mellow feel to the overall landscape. It all comes down to the effect you want to create. Bedding plant success requires good planning, bed preparation, and a solid maintenance program. Here are some basics on how to do it right.

2.5.1   Bedding Plant Selection

There are many cultivars (varieties) of bedding plants available. There's always an array of both old standard cultivars and new introductions to choose from. Selecting a wide variety of bedding plants that bloom at different times of the season is always wise, too. It keeps your customers happy and can drum up business from their impressed neighbors.

If a customer asks you about an old favorite of theirs that they used to enjoy but quit planting due to diseases or insects, give them hope. Tell them you'll see if there's a recent introduction that's more resistant. You'll probably find a good alternative! University and private plant breeders work hard to stay ahead of the game. Another good way to keep up with new introductions is to talk to suppliers and seed company representatives.

The All-America Selections program (**www.all-americaselections.org**) is an impartial source of information on how new cultivars perform in test gardens across the U.S. and Canada. If you're lucky enough to live near an All America Selections garden, or get the chance to visit one, be sure to take a look. It's a great way to become familiar with how the selections do locally and their specific characteristics. Remember too that a shady backyard on the north side of the house requires different plants than a south-facing front yard. You can also access the University of Minnesota Extension Service's online searchable plant selection criteria for hundreds of plants at **www.sustland.umn.edu/plant/index. html**.

After deciding which cultivars of bedding plants to use, buy high-quality healthy plants from a reputable nursery or garden center. Saving a few cents here and there on poor quality ones that won't make it isn't worth losing customers and your reputation over.

To your clients, instant color may be a high priority. Sometimes you have to convince them that healthy shoots and roots are more important than the number of flowers at planting time. Often, the best plants aren't the ones flowering the most in nursery flats. In the long run, your customers will be glad they took your advice.

Getting bedding plants used to a new outdoor home before you plant (called acclimation) helps ensure their success. Acclimated plants recover from transplant shock more quickly than if they were planted in the garden right away, and are healthier.

In most cases, bedding plants are pampered in a greenhouse under pretty stress-free conditions and a steady climate. It takes time to get them used to being outdoors. Give them a chance to adapt. Convince your clients that it's a good idea to let you set them outside seven to ten days before they're transplanted. Putting them in partial shade the first three to four days is also recommended. In the long run, they'll do much better if you take it slow.

2.5.2   Preparing the Soil

It's important to prepare the soil well before planting. Rake off any mulch before you till the soil and add compost or other amendments. Remember that bed preparation (especially tilling) can damage tree roots too, so be gentle.

Mixing soil amendments (organic or inorganic materials) into the soil several inches deep before you plant keeps bedding plants healthy by improving soil conditions. Properly amended clay soils will drain better and sandy soils will hold more water.

Once again I'll mention that, if you use compost, which makes a great organic amendment, make sure that it's fully decomposed. Otherwise, it will rob plants of nutrients (especially nitrogen and sulfur) and you can wind up with poor growth and maybe even a few thousand weed seeds! Whatever you decide to use, mix it in really well, using enough to equal 25% to 50% of the final soil volume.

Annual and perennial bedding plants, like all plants, need nutrients and the right pH. Before you plant them, it's a good idea to work some fertilizer into the soil and take care of any pH problems. Changing the pH is much easier before, rather than after, planting.

What should you apply and how much should you add? For large plantings, it's often a good idea to take a soil sample (after the flowerbed has been amended) and send it to a reputable lab before you plant or fertilize. You'll get the results in a couple weeks and you'll know what's actually needed. This cuts down on mistakes from guessing, which can lead to salt damage and water pollution from too much fertilizer, or poor growth from not enough.

Request tests for phosphorus, potassium, calcium, and magnesium, and find out what the pH is and if it needs adjusting. Along with the results, most labs include detailed reports telling you what kinds and rates of fertilizer to apply based on your specific results. They'll also advise you what to do, if anything, to raise or lower the pH (see the sidebar in section 2.3.3 on labs for soil testing).

The soil pH for bedding plants should be slightly on the acidic side, between 5.5 and 6.5. If you only need to check the pH and already know the nutrition level of the soil, you can do it yourself pretty easily. There are several reliable portable pH meters on the market that are easy to use and take only about 30 minutes or so from start to finish.

If the pH needs to be raised, you can mix ground limestone evenly into the top six or seven inches of the bed. To lower a high pH, elemental sulfur can be mixed into the soil. Applying an acidifying fertilizer like ammonium sulfate or ammonium nitrate is a good, cheap way to get nitrogen into the soil and reduce a high pH. It is used widely in the west for these reasons.

You're probably wondering why I haven't said anything about nitrogen. Don't all landscape plants need a lot of it? Yes! Bedding plants need more nitrogen than any other nutrient, but a soil test isn't the way to figure out how much to apply. Why? Because nitrogen is very water-soluble. It moves quickly through the water stream, not sticking around long in any one place. So, even though a soil test will tell you how much nitrogen is in the soil and how much is needed at the time the test is taken, by the time you get the results, the situation has changed. For this reason, it's best to base nitrogen applications on general recommendations rather than on results of a soil test.

You can review the material in section 2.1.2 about the difference between fast-release and slow-release fertilizers. Both kinds work fine; just follow label instructions for newly installed flowerbeds.

If you use a slow-release fertilizer, it's best to mix the first application into the bed just before planting, and spread the second half over the soil surface halfway through the season. Many slow-release fertilizers contain phosphorus and potassium as well as nitrogen and are especially formulated for bedding plants, which adds convenience.

2.5.3 Planting

Once the bed has been prepared, the real fun begins. You're ready to plant! Regardless of the "look" you want to achieve, resist the temptation to plant bedding plants around the base of trees. Keep them several inches away so they won't steal water and nutrients from the trees. That can be a no-win situation.

If you're asked to plant bedding plants in the same place where other plants were removed, find out what grew there before. This helps avoid problems that might crop up again, like soil-borne diseases. And find out which (if any) herbicides were used that may affect new plantings.

Plant the bedding plants at the same depth they were in their containers and gently tamp the amended soil firmly around the roots. Planting too deep can increase diseases, and planting too shallow weakens plants and doesn't provide enough support.

Some landscapers make preformed planting holes ahead of time to make sure the spacing is right and to save time during transplanting. This is a good idea for large beds, because it reduces the amount of time the plants go without water.

Space the transplants so the beds will be full, but not crowded, when the plants are mature. Each cultivar of bedding plant has its own spacing preference between plants based on their ultimate size when grown; follow recommendations. For variety, try a triangular spacing, which uses staggered rows with equal spacing between plants in each row to add volume to a flowerbed. The results look very professional, creating beds of beautiful, full blooms not bound by a pattern of rows. Sure, you'll need a few more plants per area, but the results are well worth it!

Mulches reduce evaporation and weeds, and improve the overall look of a flower bed. Apply them two to three inches deep between plants but only about one-half inch deep around the plants themselves to prevent disease problems. Many materials can be used: bark nuggets and chips, pine straw, and large particle compost all work well.

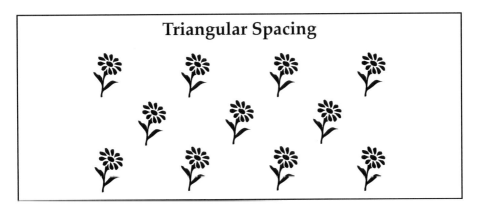

Triangular Spacing

Once the plants are in, they should be watered as soon as possible, gently and thoroughly. The beds should be kept moist, but not soggy, until they plants are well rooted. It's important not to let the roots dry out while they're getting used to their new home. You can water less often once they're established.

2.5.4   Maintenance

General Bedding Plant Maintenance

Deadheading (removing dead and wilted flowers) once a week keeps flower beds attractive, reduces the spread of diseases, and promotes flowering. Bedding plants that benefit from deadheading include celosia, coleus, dahlias, geraniums, gloriosa daisy, marigolds, salvia, and zinnia.

Many landscapers also prune certain kinds of bedding plants to keep them compact and to increase flowering. Some flowers, like gomphrena, can even be sheared into shapes. If you decide to prune, leave about half of the shoot length intact and "stagger prune." This means pruning every third plant once a week for about three weeks so you won't remove all the color from the beds. By then, the first plants you pruned should be flowering again. Stagger pruning is a common practice in petunia beds.

Preventing weeds from germinating before they become a problem is the best way to avoid an all out weed war in the flowerbed. How can you do this? First, make sure any compost you add as a soil amendment is completely broken down so any weeds seeds in it won't germinate.

Plant beds full enough to crowd out unwanted neighbors, and water and fertilize properly. You may still get a few weeds, but they can be hand pulled or carefully hoed.

Chemical pre or post-emergent herbicides are an option on large plantings of a single species of flower. Pre-emergent herbicides are applied to prevent weeds from germinating at all, and post-emergent herbicides kill already germinated weeds.

Even then, keeping plants healthy before weed problems crop up is the best practice. Herbicides aren't generally recommended to prevent or remove weeds on smaller plantings and those with lots of different types of flowers with different sensitivities to weed killers. What's best for the environment is also best for the flowerbed and, more and more, customers are requesting that pesticides be used only if absolutely necessary.

Watering

Color beds should be watered separately from trees, shrubs, and turf to make sure the right amount of water is applied at the right time to all the plants. Drip systems work great. They reduce evaporation, apply water slowly into the root zone, and keep the leaves and flowers dry which discourages diseases. Runoff is reduced since the rate that drip systems apply water is much lower than those of traditional sprinkler systems. As always, the best time to irrigate is early in the morning.

Remember earlier how I talked about how important it was for the soil to be able to take up water before it runs off and is wasted? Applying water to bedding plants slowly enough so that it can be taken up is just as important as it is with trees, lawns and any other kind of plant.

As I've explained, clay soils take up water much more slowly than sandy soils. Amending a clay soil will increase the infiltration rate, but it will always be less than that of a sandier soil. Deep tilling beds by breaking up the soil before planting can improve drainage a lot, too. Plants growing in a clay soil may need to be watered only once a week since it drains slowly. The same plants grown in a sandier soil may need to be watered every other day.

Of course, how quickly a soil dries out changes seasonally, is faster in sun than shade, and depends on the water use of the plant and the climate. Compaction and layered soils or hardpan also reduce drainage and aeration and should be taken care of before planting. Usually, adding soil amendments takes care of any problem.

Fertilizing Soil

Most annuals grow best in flower beds with regular fertilizer throughout their growing season. While nitrogen is important, remember that too much will reduce flowering and increase foliar growth, so make sure you add adequate phosphorus (the second number on a bag of fertilizer).

An application of a slow-release fertilizer once or twice during the growing season is one way to save labor when fertilizing, although the fertilizer itself costs more than a soluble one costs. A rate of about one or two pounds of slow release fertilizer per 100 square feet of garden is about right, but be sure to follow directions on the bag, since formulations vary.

As an alternative, you may use a soluble fertilizer such as 10-20-10 at the rate of one pound per 100 gallons of water, and apply it about once a month during the growing season. If you chose a dry fertilizer, remember to water it in well and spread it evenly and in a non-windy period.

Geraniums, impatiens, and some of the newer petunias are relatively heavy feeders, while nasturtium requires less fertilizer. Perennials don't require as much fertilizer as annuals since they live more than one year and don't need to grow new roots each season.

2.6 Keeping Busy All Year

It's true that landscaping work is seasonal for the most part, but as you'll read in this section, landscape company owners have developed a number of lucrative ways to keep busy when the snow flies or things turn cold. There are also some tips on caring for plants and trees in extremely cold climates.

2.6.1   Autumn Jobs

Fertilize Lawns

Fall is a great time of year to fertilize lawns. Adding too much fertilizer in early spring can result in lots of shoot growth that can deplete energy reserves going into summer. Applying fertilizer in late October or early November, when top growth is minimal but soil temperatures are still warm enough for root absorption of nitrogen, avoids this problem. It extends the time the grass is green in the fall, and generates great early color the following spring.

Clean up Perennial Beds

Every few years, perennial flowers need a little help. They've done their thing on their own up until now, but to keep them healthy for another few years, you need to give them a boost.

After they've completed their flowering for the year, carefully remove each plant from the soil, pull each section apart with your hands, and replant them several inches apart. The colder the climate, the earlier in fall you should replant them to give them time to root before winter.

You can also remove dying leaves and flowers each year in the fall. This is important before new growth starts in spring to reduce the chance of pests. Exceptions are lavender (which gets its new leaves from old stems), garden mums (you can remove old flowers but not the foliage) and evergreen perennials. Compost what you remove.

Tuck Roses In: A "Tip" from Minnesota

In cold climates, roses need to be pampered in the winter. Your reward will be beautiful blooms the next summer. Here's a method widely used in the upper Midwest, made famous in Minnesota where some real winter experts are. It's called the Minnesota Tip Method.

Stop fertilizing in mid-August but irrigate deeply well into late fall. Consider spraying plants with a fungicide to prevent spores from over-wintering — this is a case where use of a pesticide is often warranted.

Dig a trench around each plant around the last week of October. If you want, you can make it large enough to hold several plants. Tie the rose canes together in a bundle. Loosen the soil around each plant a little bit and gently bend ('tip') the ends of the bushes into the trench. Cover them with the soil you took out of the trench. When the ground is slightly frozen, cover everything with three or four inches of leaves. Wait a few days and add several inches to a foot of mulch. This keeps everything intact so it won't blow away.

In April when Minnesotans are playing tennis outdoors in their t-shirts and shorts thinking it's warm, it's time to resurrect the plants. Carefully lift them out of their hibernating caves and replace the soil around them. Don't forget to water them deeply and thoroughly.

An alternative to tipping is to tie the rose canes together in mid-October. Mound about eight inches of soil around each plant and surround it with wire netting. Fill the "container" you just made with three feet or so of fallen leaves. Add a layer of heavier mulch to keep things intact. Around tax time (April 15), remove the mound and water the plants well.

Irrigate Deeply

Trees and shrubs need to be watered deeply well into the fall for root growth.

Replenish Mulch

If the mulch layer in flower beds and around trees and shrubs is less than three or four inches thick, which can happen due to wind, decomposition, and foot traffic even if it was thick enough earlier in the year, add more. Make sure to extend it several feet out from the tree toward the dripline.

Clean Tools

Cleaning your tools before soil and debris gets caked on them will save you lots of time in the busy spring. Clean mud and dirt off shovels, forks, and trowels with soap and water. Rub some linseed oil into wood handles to prevent them from drying and cracking.

Winterize Mowers and Gas-powered Equipment

Run all your gas mowers and gas-powered tools until the gas tanks are empty. Take the spark plug out and drop a couple drops of oil in the opening before adding a new plug. Clean soil and matted grass off the blades and take them in for sharpening. Ask for that winter special!

Remove and Compost Leaves

Rake leaves that fall from deciduous trees off of turf. Collect and compost them. Leaves left on the lawn can cause disease problems because they reduce light and oxygen. In more natural settings, though, you can leave them alone.

Winterize Irrigation Systems

Once temperatures drop and fall is in the air, it's time to prepare irrigation systems for hibernation. This prevents damage in cold winter climates. Taking necessary steps to winterize them can avoid expensive repairs in spring. Even self-draining systems need to be checked. It's not worth risking it.

Removing all the water in the system is important since even a small amount can freeze, expand and crack piping, and damage the backflow assembly. There are three ways of winterizing: manual drain, auto drain, or "blowout." If you don't know what type your customer has, use the failsafe blowout method.

The manual drain method is used when manual valves are at the end and low points of the irrigation piping. Drain these systems by shutting off the water supply and opening the manual drain valves. Then, open the boiler drain valve or the drain cap on the stop and waste valve (it will be one or the other) and drain the water between the shut off valve and the backflow device. Open the test cocks on the backflow device. If there are check valves on the sprinklers, pull up the sprinklers and drain the water out the bottom. Once all the water has drained, close the manual drain valves.

The automatic drain method is used when automatic drain valves are located at the end and low points of the irrigation piping. They will automatically open and drain if the pressure in the piping is under 10 PSI.

Turn off the irrigation water supply and activate a station. After the water has drained out of the mainline, open the boiler drain valve or the drain cap on the stop and waste valve (it will be one or the other) and drain the water between the shut off valve and the backflow device. Open the test cocks on the backflow device. If there are check valves on your sprinklers, pull up the sprinklers and drain the water out the bottom.

The blowout method that should only be performed by a qualified licensed contractor. If you pursue contracting, this can be a lucrative service to offer.

2.6.2   Winter Work

Here are some chores that will keep you busy through the winter. After all, you don't want your clients to forget about you!

Prune Trees and Shrubs

Deciduous trees love winter pruning. Pruning during their winter dormancy period after leaf drop and before spring buds begin to swell is one of the best things you can do to keep them healthy. There are several advantages of winter pruning: you can see exactly what you're doing since there aren't any leaves; the frozen ground helps cushion heavy equipment, protecting turf from damage; disease pathogens are dormant; and you and your crew have more time.

In fact, winter is the only time of year that oak, apple, pear, mountain ash, hawthorn, cotoneaster and other susceptible trees should be pruned to prevent the spread of oak wilt and fire blight. Remove deadwood, broken branches, and narrow angled branches; and thin as needed, making sure you maintain the tree's natural shape. Unless you're a Certified Tree Worker or Arborist (see section 3.3 on certifications), leave work that can't be reached from the ground to a professional.

Winter is also a great time to renew and revitalize overgrown shrubs with a little pruning. Remove about one-fourth of the oldest branches all the way back to the base to stimulate new growth. This lets light in and improves air circulation, too. Healthy new growth will be your spring reward.

There are a few kinds of trees and shrubs that you shouldn't prune in winter, including conifers such as pine, cypress, juniper, and yew. They should be pruned just before their spring/early summer growth flush instead. Heavy pruning may also cause some to weaken and die. This is because pines and many other conifers don't generate new buds in old branches. Some trees, like maple, elm, birch, and dogwood, produce lots of sap when they're pruned in late winter or early spring. Although it doesn't hurt the tree itself, it can leave a sticky mess.

> **TIP:** You can also use this time to plant B&B and bare-root plants. This gives them a head start in early spring.

Snow and Ice Removal

In many parts of the cold north, landscapers routinely perform snow removal services. In fact, there's a very active trade association, the Snow and Ice Management Association (**www.sima.org**), that's growing rapidly.

The challenge for those who are new in the business is the fact that equipment and fuel costs can be expensive. But many seasoned snow removal professionals that manage their winter business add a very nice supplement to their landscape company income. The key is budgeting and knowing your costs, just like it is managing the landscape end of things.

You might discover that it's advantageous to hire good workers that you can keep on all year. That saves money hiring and retraining, and keeps the employees happy. After all, they need some winter income, too.

Supply Firewood

Sitting with a loved one nestled in front of a roaring old-fashioned fireplace is still on the top of the "How Romantic" list for many people. Other people look at the whole thing much more practically, preferring to shave off a few hundred dollars a year from their heating bills by using a wood-burning stove.

In either case, there's a demand like never before for high-quality firewood, causing the price to increase dramatically over the past ten years with no sign of slowing down. And in many areas (even including the warmer southwest) there's plenty of room for a little more competition.

Most homeowners who want firewood don't live near a forest and need someone to supply it. That's where your landscape company looking for a little winter business comes in. Consider tapping into this growing market during the off-season. It can be lucrative and satisfying.

You don't need a contractor's license to get this seasonal business going. From a safety perspective, though, you should get some training in safe techniques for using a splitter and other equipment for yourself and any employees who will be helping.

Do a little market research to find where your company best fits in. Whole logs? Split logs? Custom cut wood for fireplaces and stoves? Sawed scrap lumber? Mill ends? Once you're in the landscape business, you'll likely get to know a few arborists who can be your suppliers. If you decide to become a professional arborist yourself, this makes the job even easier and increases your profit since you won't need to hire a go-between to supply the wood. Just make sure you have a large enough source of wood to service your customers. Don't run out during a January snowstorm!

It's not unheard of to make a 10-fold profit on selling wood to your customers, according to Peter Hincks of Timberwolf Corporation. He's been marketing splitters to arborists for years, indicating that a decent quality one costs around $6,000.

Besides the obvious buying of mill ends from sawmills, Peter suggests contacting local lumberyards, woodworking or furniture manufacturing firms, and homebuilding or remodeling contractors.

He suggests: "Ask them if you can drop by about once a week and clean up their work site by hauling away scrap lumber. They might do an even swap with you at no cost. The only downside is that you'll need to sort and saw it yourself. Plastic shipping bands work great for bundling the cut wood, and the banding tool doesn't cost much. Your customers will appreciate the tight, neat stacks, and they can cut the band easily with a pair of scissors." He suggests packaging cut wood in convenient sizes for your customer's fireplaces. You can read more of his advice at **www.timberwolfcorp.com/advice/start_a_firewood_business.htm**.

You can save time and increasing company profits by hiring teenagers to prepare and stack the bundles for you. Check the time it takes two students working at a reasonably fast clip to determine a fair per-bundle wage. Then pay them per 100 bundles.

The best place to find whole logs is a sawmill or logging operation not too far away. Request that lumber rejects be delivered to your wood lot. Your costs will depend on the size and number delivered. Charge double whatever they are.

Another source of lumber is to get a permit to cut firewood in designated areas from your local Forest Service or Bureau of Land Management. Never illegally cut and remove wood without a permit, though.

States laws vary pertaining to collecting and removing down or dead wood from public lands. In Idaho, for example, you can gather firewood from the USDA Forest Service lands, Idaho Department of Lands, Forest Industry and woodlot owners. Each has their own regulations governing gathering and removal. Permits vary from no charge to fee-based. In some cases, there are restrictions on gathering wood from certain species.

Not all wood is created equally. Burn times vary, with deciduous hardwoods (oak, maple, etc.) burning slower than birches. Many homeowners don't want to burn conifers due to the fact that they produce creosote when oxygen-starved or burned wet.

Be careful not to remove trees providing an active habitat for birds or mammals, even if the trees are dead. Check with your state Forest Service or Cooperative Extension Forester for specifics. If you buy land from a private landowner, make sure you get a receipt as proof of origination. Follow all chainsaw and fire safety laws to the T!

You may need to do some educating to let your customers know that firs, hemlocks and pines are often more plentiful than hardwoods, and work very well for home use under the right conditions. Stay away from cedars; they're not a good choice. Also, some trees burn hotter than others. Western larch and Douglas fir put out lots of heat, while spruce puts out less.

In the business, fuelwood usually sells by the cord (128 cubic feet), which stacks four feet high, four feet wide, and eight feet long. To haul a cord, you'd need more than a half-ton truck. Most residential customers will order much less (one-third to one-half cord) at a time.

Cut and remove logs in eight-foot lengths, load them into your vehicle and haul them to your woodlot. Before you get too carried away, think about where you're going to store your loot. You'll probably need at least half an acre.

If you offer full service, consider letting customers choose their own logs from your site. Charge them twice your cost, then $10 for every log you saw into desired lengths for them, $10 for splitting it, and another $10 for loading the split wood into their vehicle. Peter indicated that this kind of full-service operation can net $100 an hour, especially if you hire students to help.

Before you move too fast, make sure you have the right equipment. Minimally, you should have a good quality log splitter. If you decide to grow this end of your business, you might want to consider buying your own wood processor, or hire that part out.

I suggest that you offer a 10% to 20% discount to faithful residential landscape customers for their continued business in the off-season. Mail flyers to all your customers in late summer (or enclose them with your bill) letting them know you can also supply their firewood needs.

Try to drum up business in entire neighborhoods, offering sizable discounts when several people from a single neighborhood go in together on a full truck of wood. Many of them will probably prefer that you deliver the final cut product to their home rather than them having to pick it up.

Offer to deliver individual allotments to each homeowner at set intervals throughout the winter; this lets you give them an even deeper discount without cutting into your profit since your travel expenses and time on the road are reduced. To do this most effectively, you should either mail flyers to each address in a several block area, or put on a company shirt and make the rounds yourself. Any new customers you pick up are excellent candidates for landscape services the next season.

Once you've got your seasonal firewood supply business on a profitable footing and running smoothly, you might even want to offer firewood accessories and woodstoves.

Christmas Trees and Holiday Decoration Set Up

Homeowners have busier schedules than ever before. While selecting a choose-and-cut Christmas tree can be a great family activity, actually getting a large one home and setting it up can be a problem. Not everyone has a large enough vehicle, while others just don't want to take the time.

Offering a tree delivery and set up service can be a great way to extend your landscape business into the winter and can also drum up business for spring. When the season's all over, consider getting together with local arborists and offering a free tree pick up and composting service. You'll be in the perfect position to reap the rewards by stockpiling valuable organic matter for use as mulch and soil amendment during the season.

In addition to needing someone to deliver and set up their Christmas trees, more and more busy urbanites are hiring out tree and house decorating services, as well. If you're not the most artistic person, it's another great opportunity to hire high school and college students on winter break to decorate the trees and houses for you. Make sure someone's insurance is going to cover any falls off the top eaves of the house, though!

Interiorscaping

Interiorscaping (taking care of potted plants in homes and office buildings) is another off-season add-on that more and more landscape companies are including as a service. Some companies specialize in interiorscaping year-round, which is another growing business opportunity.

Just as outdoor plants provide many environmental and health-related benefits, interior plants also remove certain toxins from the air and improve air quality. Bringing nature indoors can add a calming element to an otherwise sterile indoor environment.

Over the past several years, new and improved cultivars of interior plants have hit the market. Also, plants that used to be confined to exterior environments have been bred for interior qualities, offering many more possibilities and diversity than interiorscapes of a decade ago. Many office complexes, restaurants and homes are showing off a lot more these days than just dracaeneas and aglaonemas.

As with outdoor plants, watering is high on the list of importance. These days there are a number of new innovations, such as drip irrigation, pressurized water tanks holding several gallons of water, and even self-watering cans, which save you from having to check each account on a daily basis.

If you are interested in pursuing this specialization, contact the Plantscape Industry Alliance at **www.cipaweb.org** or (707) 462-2276 for more information.

2.6.3 Protection from Harsh Climates

I lived in Minnesota for many years and know all about harsh climates. While a fresh crop of snow beckons skiers and is an awesome sight, extreme winter conditions can cause severe damage to landscape plants.

Trees and shrubs can't get decked out in down jackets and warm boots the way we can. Winter sun, wind, and low temperatures can dry out needles, damage bark, and injure or kill entire plants. The weight of ice and snow alone can snap branches and topple trees. Even salt, the northern staple for de-icing streets and sidewalks, can harm landscape plants.

Then there are those hungry rodents just trying to make it through the winter themselves by chomping on plant parts. They can be a real force to contend with, injuring and sometimes killing their fair share of trees and shrubs.

Okay, I know this sounds like the Apocalypse. It's not so bad, really. Well-chosen hardy plants are remarkably resilient and able to withstand extremely severe winter conditions. Long, cold northern winters should not be a deterrent to planting and enjoying beautiful landscape plants. And plant breeders are constantly improving winter hardiness of many tree and shrub species.

So, how do even the hardiest plants survive cold climates like Minnesota, the upper northeast and much of Canada? It's true that roots don't go dormant in the winter very quickly, and are killed at temperatures at or below 0° to +10° F.

The key to their survival is that soil temperatures are much higher than air temperatures and cool down more slowly. Snow cover and mulch buffer soil temperatures, too, keeping them relatively high. And, since moist soil holds more heat than dry soil, soil temperatures are coldest in sandy or dry soils and warmest in clay soils.

To encourage fall root growth and to reduce root injury, newly planted trees and shrubs should be mulched with six to eight inches of wood chips or straw. Hardy plants that are watered, fertilized, pruned and wrapped properly usually do just fine through a tough winter.

Proper plant selection is the single-most important way to reduce all types of winter injury. Plant ornamentals that are hardy in your region. That means that tropical plants that thrive during a San Diego winter probably aren't high on the recommended list for January in Minnesota.

Also, remember that even hardy plants may not make it through an extreme winter. Injury is worse when lower-than-average temperatures occur in early fall or late spring, when there is below-average snow cover, when low temperatures last a long time; and when there are large fluctuations during a short period of time in fall, winter, or spring.

Let plants "harden off" by not applying large applications of nitrogen fertilizers in late summer, and don't underestimate the advantages of a good mulch! Remember to keep it several inches away from tree trunks and spread it outwards toward the dripline. Mulch applied around the bases of root-tender plants like roses (or covering them completely using the Minnesota tip method) is also a good idea.

Pruning following recommended practices helps strengthen trees and promotes good health. A well-pruned tree is able to withstand heavy snow and ice loads better than a weak, poorly pruned tree.

If an evergreen has suffered winter injury, don't prune out the damage until well into spring. Leaf buds may survive. If they don't, prune dead branches back to live tissue. Fertilize injured plants in early spring and water them well throughout the season. Provide appropriate protection the following winter.

Common Winter Injuries and Controls

Here are some common winter injuries and ways you can avoid or minimize damage.

Sunscald

Problem:	Winter sunscald causes long, sunken areas of dead bark, usually on the south or southwest side of a tree. It happens when tree bark warmed during the day from the sun cools down quickly after sunset. Young trees, newly planted trees, and thin-barked trees like cherry, honey locust, linden, maple, and plum are most likely to suffer, as well as trees with exposed lower trunks. Older trees seem to fare better.
Control:	Sunscald can usually be prevented by wrapping the trunk with tree wrap, tree guard, or light-colored material. The wrap reflects the sun and keeps the bark at a steadier temperature. Apply it in the fall and take it off again in the spring after the chance of frost is over. Newly planted trees should be wrapped for at least two winters, and thin-barked species five winters or more. You can repair old damage by carefully cutting the dead bark back to live tissue. If you do this, make sure you wrap the trunk during the winter to prevent more damage.

Winter Discoloration

Problem: Winter discoloration of evergreens, also called winter desiccation or winter burn, causes leaves to turn brown during late fall and winter and occurs for many reasons. Usually, it's because water is lost through the leaves faster than it can be taken up from frozen soil. It's common during sunny and/or windy winter weather. Leaves and needles of affected broadleaves and conifers become partially or totally brown, depending how bad they are injured. Damage shows up on the south, southwest, and windward sides of a plant.

Control: Proper plant choice and placement are the keys to prevention. Pines are fairly resistant. Yew, hemlock, and arborvitae should not be planted on south or southwest sides of buildings or in windy or sunny locations. You can also reduce damage by watering plants thoroughly through the growing season and into late fall. Placing a burlap barrier around or over plants (leaving the top open for air flow and light) helps reduce windy conditions and may also help. You can protect smaller plants by wrapping burlap around four wood stakes placed around the plants, with each corner stapled. Large shrubs benefit from a two-sided, V-shaped windbreak pointed to the south, southwest or into prevailing winds from other directions.

Frost Cracks

Problem: Frost cracks are splits in the bark caused from a rapid drop in temperature. They occur more often if there has been previous injury to the trunk. Sometimes you can even hear a loud snap! Frost cracks may close and callus over during the summer but reopen again in the winter.

Control: Be careful not to wound tree bark with mowers, weed whips, and other equipment. That's how most frost cracks start. Placing mulch around young trees helps prevent frost cracks indirectly by adding a barrier between the tree and the grass that reduces the chance of equipment injury. Mulches provide many other benefits to the plants, as well. You can brace large frost "ribs" so they won't reopen during winter. Since frost cracks invite wood-decaying organisms, check affected trees often to make sure they're not a hazard due to this type of decay.

Frost Heaving

Problem   Frost heaving can expose roots of newly transplanted trees and small shrubs to cold aboveground temperature, wind, and sun. When this results in lots of freezing and drying, plants may eventually die.

Control   Proper mulching around the base and root zone of plants will greatly reduce the chance of freezing and thawing, which causes most frost heaving problems. If you notice injury during the winter, wait until spring to determine how bad it is, replace dead plants, and mulch the new transplants.

Snow and Ice Damage

Problem   Heavy snow and ice can cause lots of damage to trees, especially if the soil is saturated before a storm. If too much weight is placed on the upper portion of a tree, the root system can even be pulled completely out of the ground. The usual damage is bending and breaking branches.

Control   Properly prune trees and shrubs to eliminate weak branches. Leave branches with wide angles since they are usually stronger than those with narrow angles. Plant trees and shrubs away from overhangs and roofs where melting snow can fall on them, freezing later on. You can also cover small shrubs with temporary wood barriers. Small trees can be wrapped together or the leaders tied with strips of carpet, strong cloth or nylon stockings. Just remember to remove the wrap in spring! Proper pruning that removes multiple leaders and weak branches will reduce snow and ice damage. For trees with large wide-spreading leaders or large multistemmed trees, the main branches should be cabled together by a professional arborist.

Salt Damage

Problem   Salt used for de-icing roads and sidewalks can result in winter injury and dieback.

Control   To prevent damage, an obvious answer is to avoid planting trees and shrubs close to areas that are de-iced or collect runoff from it. If your client asks you to protect a tree already subject to damage, a burlap barrier may help.

Rodents and Deer

Problem   Rodents and deer often enjoy quite a winter feast, at the plant's expense! They gorge on twigs, bark, and foliage, girdling trees and mowing shrubs to the ground. Deer can also cause lots of damage by rubbing their antlers on trees during the fall.

Control   You can protect trees from rodent damage by putting a cylinder of ¼" mesh hardware cloth around the trunk, extending two to three inches below the ground for mice and 18 to 24 inches above the expected snow line for rabbit protection. The cloth can be left on year-round, but make sure that it is allows for tree growth. Small trees often do fine with plastic tree guards, and shrubs can escape rabbits' damage with some chicken-wire fencing.

Rodent and deer repellents work, too, and may be a viable alternative for large plantings. These don't kill or harm snooping animals; they just have offensive tastes or smells. If you have to get out heavy arsenal, there are commercial baits containing poisoned grain labeled for rodent control. I don't generally recommend them because they contain chemicals that can harm humans, pets, and beneficial wildlife. By all means, if you do use them, keep them stored away from children, well labeled, and only use them on targeted rodents. Deer can also be kept at bay with high fencing.

3. Develop Your Skills

Every profession requires certain skills. I've worked closely with successful landscape company owners for several years and see the same recipe over and over for why some make it and some don't. Their viewpoint regarding why they've become so successful is similar to mine.

Here are important skills I'm convinced will lead you right down the road to success. I'm not going to number them, because I think they're equally important.

- Good interpersonal and communication skills

- Solid horticulture knowledge

- A strong work ethic

- Planning and organizational skills

- Strength, endurance, and flexibility

- Basic math, reading, and writing skills

- Basic mechanical skills

While you need a basic grasp of these skills by the time you open up shop, remember that honing these skills is a career-long process and you don't ever have to be a jack of all trades.

Few successful landscape company owners start out with evenly balanced skills. What is important for keeping your business afloat is knowing your strengths and weaknesses. If you've got the greenest thumb in town, but aren't so strong in the business side of things, plan on getting help in this area, especially when it comes to business planning.

While you'll probably be hitting the mark deciding what services you're most qualified to offer (the first part of the plan), you should think about hiring out bookkeeping, tax and legal help on down the line if it's not your cup of tea. There are lots of trustworthy and qualified resources out there to help, including some great sources of online business and accounting forms.

What else does it take to make it as a landscape company owner? A true enjoyment of being outside (at times in inclement weather); physical work that can be difficult and requires strength (the ability to lift 50 or more pounds with ease); computer skills; writing skills (for correspondence, promotion and contracts); punctuality and the ability to meet deadlines; and organization so things don't fall through the cracks.

3.1 Work for a Landscape Company

I highly recommend getting as much experience and training as possible working for a reputable landscape company before starting your own business. The knowledge you will pick up for running your business by working for someone else is invaluable.

To break into the landscape industry in preparation for starting your own company, you don't need a college degree. But, to run a successful business, you'll need knowledge and skills in plant care, equipment use and safety, and business practices.

Even if you end up specializing in one area, having a good foundation in all facets of the business is important. For instance, understanding how a lawnmower can damage trees and the impact of shade from a tree on turf is important knowledge for you to have.

As an example, a prominent California lawncare company owner told me that on more than one occasion he prevented major damage to a client's property by pointing out dangerous, unstable trees. Even though this was not specifically his role, he was able to provide references for local certified arborists to these valued customers, who followed through, seeking this expert advice.

> **TIP:** Training also counts toward the required experience you'll need to be eligible to take certification and licensing exams to become a Certified Tree Worker, Certified Arborist, Licensed Contractor, or other specialist.

The more experience you gain before venturing out on your own, the better chance you'll have of succeeding in this field. That's why I recommend at least two seasons of experience. Since the pay is better than most entry-level horticulture jobs such as working at a nursery or garden center, and there is a strong demand for more workers in the landscape profession, it's not the hardship it is in other industries.

There are many successful companies that started out in less time by relying on bringing an experienced landscaper or two onboard as an employee, or on a contract basis. If you're particularly gifted as a business person, this approach can work quite well.

3.1.1 Applying for Work

Here is a hodgepodge of some actual classified ads that list work for landscaping positions. Not all will have the same characteristics, but this list will give you a general idea of what to expect from some of the higher-paying entry-level landscaping jobs.

Job Description

- Mow, water, weed, edge, and mulch lawns; water and weed trees and shrubs

- Remove trash, litter, and leaves; operate hand and walk behind power tools

- Operate all grounds vehicles including large trucks, forklift, and sweeper

- Operate landscape equipment such as chain saw and brush chipper
- Apply fertilizer; install sod; plant lawns, flowers, trees and shrubs
- Set up, operate, and monitor the irrigation system
- Use a computer to communicate with customers via email

Requirements

- At least 18 years old
- Valid driver's license and clean record
- Physical ability to do heavy lifting and shovel snow
- Speak English fluently
- Pass a drug screen and background check
- Basic computer competency
- Available to work any and all work schedules

Seeking These Characteristics

- Experience or a strong interest in plants and trees
- Desire to learn, grow, and advance in career
- Appreciation for outdoor work
- Positive attitude and confidence
- Honest
- Hard work and self-motivation
- Safety-focused
- Strong customer service awareness

Pay and Bonuses

- $500 - $700 weekly (one example only)

- Base pay plus weekly bonuses and commission

- Medical/dental/life insurance

- 401(k) plan

- Paid vacation & holidays

- Year-round employment

- Tuition reimbursement

- Employee stock ownership

As you can see, these jobs don't require anything beyond high school education, and some even provide educational opportunities. What employers are looking for are applicants who have a positive attitude, aren't afraid of hard work, and are willing and eager to learn. Sound like you? Working as a team player and taking a personal interest in the company are mentioned time and time again as ways you can out-compete others when it comes to getting your foot in the door, too.

You probably won't get hired as a grounds manager, crew foreman, or supervisor without a few years of experience and at least one certificate and/or license — in fact, in many states, these are required. But, if you want to be your own boss and own your own landscape company, this probably isn't your goal anyway.

Instead, focus on getting as much overall experience in as many facets of the landscape field as possible from a well-respected company. Beginning with the foundations provides diversity and lets you get a better idea of what services you want to offer once you start up your own company.

There is at least one job board for finding landscape work. PLANET (Professional Landcare Network) has a job board where you can search for landscaping jobs or post your resume. Careers listed in this job board for people new to the business include crewperson, maintenance, applicator, etc. They also have internships listed in their search area. You can find the job board at **http://careers.landcarenetwork.org/search/**. You can also try more conventional job boards such as Monster, Yahoo! HotJobs, Jobster, Job Shark, and so on, using the search terms found at the PLANET job board.

3.1.2   Getting the Most out of the Experience

Apply for jobs with companies that are truly professional. This can be a large, medium, or small company, nationally based or local. What is important are the quality of services offered, and the expertise of the workforce.

Check credentials, just as you will respect a potential client asking about yours down the line. Does the owner or a key employee belong to at least one professional association/society? Are they licensed and certified in areas they perform work in?

For instance, a reputable tree care company will not only meet the minimum standards of being licensed and insured, but will also belong to the International Society of Arboriculture and have at least one Certified Tree Worker or Certified Arborist on staff.

Many landscape company owners have a harder time finding motivated employees willing to start with the basics than they do finding supervisory and mid-management employees, whom they often hire from within. They'll more often than not respect your game plan and be glad they're hiring such an ambitious person. Look at this job opportunity as a paid internship.

Debra Amerson, mentioned in section 2.1.5 earlier in this guide, who owns an award-winning, installation and plant care service located in Marin County, California, takes this advice a step further:

> "If you can afford to, consider volunteering at a company you really respect rather than taking a paid position. Often, you'll get a lot more insider information, experience and respect from the owners this way. I open my doors at Plantris to this and I've done it myself."

Hey, it beats a required doctor's residency with double the hours and full-time stress! Use this opportunity to learn as much as you can about estimating job costs, keeping the books, and staying on the legal side of Uncle Sam, as well as how to grow the healthiest plants in town.

When you're looking for that initial landscape job to get experience in the field, trump up education if that's your stronghold, and work experience if that's more of a strength. If you have some college or vocational training under your belt (maybe quite a lot if you're making a mid-career job change), use this to your advantage, even if it's in a completely different field.

Classes that may not even seem important anymore, like that Greek Art class you took to impress your girlfriend, show that you value learning. But above all, remember that while having some post-secondary education and some experience may raise your qualifications, a good attitude and a willingness to learn are, at minimum, just as important to a potential employer.

The landscape world can be small, and being honest and upfront are virtues that are highly respected by others. When you're interviewing for a landscape job to get experience, don't promise to stay with the company forever unless you're actually considering working your way up the company ladder.

I know this may sound like questionable advice, but integrity is important, in everything you pursue in life. In the long run, you will benefit from this, and can hold your head high when you're networking with your former boss a few years later at an association meeting or even on a job site.

If you eventually open up a company specializing in landscape lighting or irrigation, your ex-boss is much more likely to have you on the top of his/her referral list for clients in need of the services you offer if you're remembered as a ambitious, hard-working person of integrity.

3.2   Formal and Informal Education

A college degree isn't required for you to open up your own landscape company. If you wanted to, you could start right away without a single course. You won't get hauled off to prison like you would if you hung out your "doctor" shingle with no degree. But if you want to be on the cutting edge of the profession, you'll look at education in a broader sense as something that can be beneficial to your personal and professional growth.

There are many routes to take. The one you choose should depend on your short and long-term goals and be paced with getting your company up and running. Of course if you offer services other than lawn and garden care, such as major tree pruning and any pest control, you'll need certificates and licenses as well.

3.2.1   Courses and Seminars

University Cooperative Extension

Cooperative Extension is the outreach arm of your state land grant university system in partnership with federal (United States Department of Agriculture) and county resources. There is a state-by-state list of contact information for university Cooperative Extension departments at the end of this guide you can refer to.

You may consider taking land grant university Cooperative Extension classes in tree care, lawn maintenance, irrigation management, pest identification and control, and/or business. You don't need any prior college to take these courses. They are stand-alone (not leading to a degree) and are oriented specifically toward meeting educational goals of employed professionals, or aspiring ones. They are taught by university and industry leaders.

The information you'll acquire is known for its credibility, practicality, and low cost — often only $25 to $75 for a full-day class that includes hand-outs, a coffee break, and even lunch!

Another great thing about these classes is that they usually offer continuing education hours to fulfill certification/license requirements you might have. Often, you can earn hours from the Irrigation Association (IA), International Society of Arboriculture (ISA), or state Department of Pesticide Regulations (DPR), all at the same seminar.

Vocational and Community Colleges

If you have always dreamed of earning a vocational, community college, four-year, or even graduate-level degree, go for it! Hundreds of vocational and community colleges in the United States and Canada offer certificates and degrees in horticulture, often with specialties in turf management, landscape management, or arboriculture.

Now is also the time to consider taking some classes or getting a minor in business administration. The National Center for Education Statistics lists hundreds of post-secondary vocational, technical, college and university programs offering training in horticulture (under agriculture), natural resources, biology and related fields. You can find out more at **http://nces.ed.gov/globallocator**.

University Extension or Continuing Education Courses

Many Universities offer Extension (different from Cooperative Extension) courses leading to certificates in many fields, including landscaping and business. You don't need to formally apply through an academic chain of command to take these courses (i.e., no one is going to ask you what your high school GPA was).

For example, University of California, Riverside Extension offers two-year certificate programs in landscape management, turfgrass management, and landscape irrigation, and University of California, Los Angeles Extension offers a certificate in landscape design.

More and more of these courses are offered online in "real time" so you can log on from your home computer and see as well as hear the instructor, and participate in class discussions. Many are offered during the evening, tailor-made for those who are working during the day.

Take advantage of these excellent opportunities to keep on top of cutting-edge practical knowledge, and to meet and network with other professionals in your field. It's a great way to stay current on everything from pest problems and equipment advances to new plants, and to be seen as a rising leader in your profession.

3.2.2   Study Landscaping on your own

Cooperative Extension Publications

Besides coursework mentioned above, Cooperative Extension offers thousands of free or low-cost fact sheets and publications written for professionals by academics with applied off-campus field expertise. You can download and print what you need. Some examples of free downloadable Cooperative Extension publications in landscaping and related fields include:

- *University of Arizona Cooperative Extension*
  Firewise Plant Materials for 3,000 ft. and Higher Elevations, by Tom DeGomez, Jeff Schalau, and Chris Jones (2002)
  http://ag.arizona.edu/pubs/natresources/az1289.pdf

- *University of California Cooperative Extension*
  Pest Notes. Lawn Diseases: Prevention and Management, by J. Hartin, P. Giesel, and A. Harivandi (2002)
  http://anrcatalog.ucdavis.edu/TurfLawns/7497.aspx

- *Kansas State University Extension*
  Turfgrass Mowing: Professional Series, by Matthew J. Fagerness and Jack Frey (2001)
  www.oznet.ksu.edu/library/hort2/samplers/mf2129.asp

- *Virginia Cooperative Extension*
  Mowing To Recycle Grass Clippings: Let the Clips Fall Where They May! by David R. Chalmers and Judy Booze-Daniels (2000)
  www.ext.vt.edu/pubs/turf/430-402/430-402.html

Contact the Cooperative Extension office serving your state (listed at the end of this guide) for a free publication catalog, or log onto their website for instant access to hundreds of free publications.

Green Industry Associations

Join at least one! Most have local chapters, which offer lots of opportunities to get acquainted with other professionals in your area and keep up on local issues.

Dan Foley, former president of the PLANET Association (listed below), has the following to say about the value of joining associations:

"I recommend that anyone who is interested in owning their landscape or lawn care company consider the many resources that local and national associations can provide. An association can provide the traditional resources

such as publications, training tools, tradeshows, educational seminars, up-dates on industry issues and trends etc. In addition, the networking and sharing of 'best practices' can provide amazing benefits that shorten the learning curve and help new companies to get established and grow."

- *American Society of Horticulture Science*
  Address: 113 South West Street, Suite 200
                   Alexandria, VA 22314-2851
  Phone: (703) 836-4606
  Website: **www.ashs.org**

- *The American Nursery & Landscape Association (ANLA)*
  Address: 1000 Vermont Avenue, NW, Suite 300
                   Washington, DC 20005-4914
  Phone: (202) 789-2900
  Website: **www.anla.org**

- *The Irrigation Association*
  Address: 6540 Arlington Boulevard
                   Falls Church, VA 22042-6638
  Phone: (703) 536-7080
  Website: **www.irrigation.org**

- *US Composting Council*
  Address: 4250 Veterans Memorial Highway, Suite 275
                   Holbrook, NY 11741
  Phone: (631) 737-4931
  Website: **www.compostingcouncil.org**

- *International Society of Arboriculture*
  Address: P.O. Box 3129
                   Champaign, IL 61826-3129
  Phone: (217) 355-9411
  Website: **www.isa-arbor.com**

- *Irrigation and Green Industry*
  Address: ISG Communications, Inc.
                   6925 Canby Avenue, Suite 1102
                   Reseda, CA 91335
  Phone: (818) 342-3204
  Website: **http://igin.com**

- *Professional Landcare Network (PLANET)*
  Address: 950 Herndon Parkway, Suite 450
             Herndon, VA 20179
  Phone: 1 (800) 395-2522
  Website: **www.landcarenetwork.org**

- *Snow and Ice Management Association*
  Address: 7670 North Port Washington Rd., Suite 105
             Milwaukee, WI 53217
  Phone: (414) 375-1940
  Website: **www.sima.org**

- *Sports Turf Managers Association*
  Address: 805 New Hampshire, Ste. E
             Lawrence, KS 66044
  Phone: 1 (800) 323-3875
  Website: **www.stma.org**

Magazines

- *Arbor Age (Green Media Online)*
  Phone: (770) 995-4964
  Website: **www.greenmediaonline.com**

- *Arborist News (through membership with ISA)*
  Phone: (217) 355-9411
  Website: **www.isa-arbor.com**

- *Grounds Maintenance*
  Phone: 1 (866) 505-7173
  Website: **http://grounds-mag.com**

- *Landscape & Irrigation (Green Media Online)*
  Phone: (770) 995-4964
  Website: **www.greenmediaonline.com**

- *Landscape Construction Magazine*
  Phone: (802) 748-8908
  Website: **www.lcmmagazine.com**

- *Landscape Contractor National*
  Address: Landscape Superintendent & Maintenance Professional
               14771 Plaza Drive, Ste. M
               Tustin, CA 92780
  Phone: (714) 979-5276
  Website: **www.landscapeonline.com/subscriptions**

- *Landscape Management*
  (Free subscription for professionals)
  Phone: 1 (888) 527-7008
  Website: **www.landscapemanagement.net/landscape**

- *Lawn and Landscape Magazine*
  Address: Editorial & Sales Offices
               4020 Kinross Lakes Parkway, Suite 201
               Richfield, OH 44286
  Phone: (800) 456-0707
  Website: **www.lawnandlandscape.com**

- *Southwest Trees & Turf*
  Address: PO Box 12507
               Las Vegas, NV 89112-0507
  Phone: (702) 454-3057
  Website: **www.swtreesandturf.com**

- *SportsTurf (Green Media Online)*
  Phone: (770) 995-4964
  Website: **www.greenmediaonline.com**

- *Tree Services Magazine*
  (Free subscription!)
  Phone: (802) 748-8908
  Website: **www.treeservicesmagazine.com**

- *Turf Magazine*
  Phone: (802) 748-8908
  Website: **www.turfmagazine.com**

Online Resources

You can find valuable information on landscape events and timely topics at **www.greenmediaonline.com** and **http://progardenbiz.com**.

Books and CDs

The ☞ indicates must-haves! In addition to the Amazon links provided, most are available from the International Society of Arboriculture (**www.isa-arbor.com**). If you join, you'll get a hefty discount on merchandise purchased through their web store.

Tree and Shrub Care

> ☞ *Arboriculture: Integrated Management of Landscape Trees, Shrubs, and Vines,*
> by Richard W. Harris, James R. Clark and Nelda P. Matheny

- *Arborists' Certification Study Guide*
  Can purchase singularly, or with an Audio CD to complement the written guide. Published by the International Society of Arboriculture.

> ☞ *An Illustrated Guide to Pruning,*
> by Edward Gilman

- *Introduction to Arboriculture: Tree Worker Safety (CD)*
  Introduction to Arboriculture: Tree Biology (CD)
  Both of these CDs supplement the certification study guide in preparation for taking the exam and obtaining continuing education units.

- *Manual of Woody Landscape Plants,*
  by Michael A. Dirr

- *Native Trees for North American Landscapes,*
  by Guy Sternberg

- *A Photographic Guide to the Evaluation of Hazard Trees in Urban Areas,*
  by Nelda P. Matheny, James R. Clark

- *Plant Health Care for Woody Ornamentals: A Professional's Guide to Preventing & Managing Environmental Stresses & Pests,* by John Lloyd

Lawn and Garden Care

- *HORTICOPIA A-Z (CD),* by Edward Gilman and Robert Lyons

- *Compendium of Turfgrass Diseases,* by Richard W. Smiley

☞ *Lawn Care for Dummies,* by Lance Walheim

- *Manual of Herbaceous Ornamental Plants,* by Steven Still

- *Pests and Diseases for Herbaceous Perennials,* by Stanton Gill, David Clement, and Ethel Dutky

- *HORTICOPIA® Expert Notes (CD)*

☞ *Turfgrass Management,* by A.J. Turgeon

General Landscape

- *Designing the Landscape: An Introductory Guide,* by Tony Bertauski

- *Professional Landscape Management,* by David L. Hensley

- *Western Fertilizer Handbook (2nd Horticulture Edition)*

Sunset (**www.oxmoorhouse.com/category/garden/regional+gardening.do**) produces the following highly recommended regional guides:

☞ *Western Garden Book*

☞ *Western Landscaping Book*

☞ *Gardening in the Northwest*

☞ *Gardening in the Southwest*

☞ *Midwestern Landscaping Book*

☞ *Northeastern Landscaping Book*

Business

☞ *Business Principles of Landscape Contracting,* by Steven M. Cohan

- *Small Business for Dummies (2nd Edition),* by Eric Tyson and Jim Schell

Canada-Specific Resources

Agriculture and Agri-Food Canada offers a program very similar to the United States Cooperative Extension Service. Its purpose is to "provide information, research and technology, and policies and programs to achieve security of the food system, health of the environment and innovation for growth." There is an extensive online searchable index.

- *Agriculture and Agri-Food Canada*
  Address: Public Information Request Services
  Sir John Carling Building
  930 Carling Ave
  Ottawa, ON K1A 0C7
  Phone: (613) 759-1000
  Website: **www.agr.gc.ca**

In addition to the associations previously listed that welcome Canadian memberships, here are some specific resources of particular relevance to Canadian landscape professionals.

- *Canadian Nursery Landscape Association*
  Address: 7856 Fifth Line South, RR#4, Station Main
  Milton, ON L9T 2X8
  Phone: (905) 875-1399 or 1-888-446-3499 (toll-free)
  Website: **www.canadanursery.com**

- *Composting Council of Canada*
  Address: 16 Northumberland Street
              Toronto, ON M6H 1P7
  Phone: (416) 535-0240 or 1 (877) 571-4769 (toll-free)
  Website: **http://compost.org**

- *Weed Control in Landscape and Turf Areas*
  A 42-page free booklet published by the Manitoba Agriculture, Food and Rural Initiatives Soils & Crops Branch. Call (204) 745-5660 to order, or visit website to download. **www.gov.mb.ca/agriculture/crops/cropproduction/ gaa01d30.html**

- *Fact Sheets on Turf and Landscape Topics*
  Available from the Ministry of Agriculture, Food and Rural Affairs
  www.omafra.gov.on.ca/english/crops/hort/turf.html#landscape

3.3   Obtaining Certification

Listed in this section are associations and organizations that offer high-quality certification programs, along with a description of each. These are all strictly voluntary, and independent from requirements pertaining to becoming a landscape contractor (see section 4.4.3 on licensing).

Becoming certified in at least one area is really a good idea. It shows other professionals and potential customers that you have the necessary training and skills in your area of specialty to perform the work, and aren't just settling for meeting the legal minimum standards.

3.3.1   Professional Landcare Network (PLANET)

PLANET is a relatively new organization combining the expertise of the Associated Landscape Contractors of America and the Professional Lawn Care Association of America. PLANET offers several certification programs developed to meet international standards. Local administration is handled through state landscape contractor association offices. Their website is located at **www.landcarenetwork.org/cms/home.html** or you can call 1-800-395-2522.

Says former president Dan Foley:

> "The Professional Landcare Network (PLANET) is an international association serving lawn care professionals, exterior landscape maintenance contractors, install/design/build contractors and interior plantscapers. PLANET provides its members with a good business foundation to help them evaluate, plan and better manage their companies. Member firms have direct access to marketing tools, industry-specific business publications, updates on legislative issues, and networking opportunities that can assist them in becoming more profitable."

To become a Certified Landscape Professional you must be a landscape company owner or manager, and pass a four-hour multiple choice exam on subjects pertinent to running a successful business. Topics cover horticulture, strategic planning, marketing, and financial management. PLANET provides the necessary study materials.

To become a Certified Landscape Technician you need to pass a hands-on field test administered by your local state or regional contractors' association. Tests are offered in several states and Canadian provinces. Components include a "Common Elements" and a "Core" test covering modules including installation and maintenance, and in some regions, irrigation.

To become a Certified Ornamental Landscape Professional you need to pass two tests covering a 20-chapter book that you can obtain through PLANET. The certification takes about a year to complete. Woody plant (tree and shrub) establishment and maintenance, soils and water management, pest identification and control, cultural and environmental problems, and pesticide safety are covered.

To become a Certified Turfgrass Professional you need to enroll in Principles of Turfgrass Management, a self-study distance education course covering all aspects of turfgrass growth and management pertinent to all of the United States, offered through the University of Georgia. You have one year to complete the program. Required proctored exams may be taken at a college or university in your area.

To become a Certified Turfgrass Professional (Cool Season Lawns) you need to enroll in a self-study distance education course especially oriented at effective turf management in colder, northern climates, with

Pennsylvania State University. You have one year to complete the program. Required proctored exams may be taken at a college or university in your area.

3.3.2   International Society of Arboriculture (ISA)

The ISA is respected world-wide for setting a premier standard for professional tree care, and more and more consumers are aware of the importance of this distinction. Of course, you'll by law need to be licensed and insured to run a tree service in most states, too.

If you're going to specialize in tree care (arboriculture), I strongly recommend that you start preparing yourself to take the International Society of Arboriculture (ISA) Certified Tree Worker or Certified Arborist exam as soon as possible. For more information, call (217) 355-9411 or visit **www.isa-arbor.com**.

To become a Certified Tree Worker you'll need at least 18 months' experience in tree care (including climbing), and then need to pass knowledge and skills exams. To become a Certified Arborist you'll need at least three years' experience in tree care (landscaping and nursery work qualify, too) and then need to pass a written exam covering all aspects of tree care.

You can keep going if you want and specialize even more as you get more experience. Recently, ISA added the following Specialist Categories. Each requires an initial credential as a Certified Arborist.

- Certified Utilities Specialist

- Certified Municipal Specialist

- Board Certified Master Arborist

To maintain your ISA certification, you need 30 hours of continuing education (CEUs) every three years. There are lots of opportunities to acquire these hours. ISA chapters across the United States and Canada sponsor many courses, as does Cooperative Extension and many of the larger tree care companies.

In addition, ISA offers credit for watching approved videos, taking accredited college classes, and participating in approved online courses.

You can earn 10 CEUs per credit hour for taking a college class from an accredited institution.

3.3.3   Irrigation Association (IA)

The IA offers certification in several specialty areas. Dr. David Zoldoske, former president, offers this advice:

> *"Professionalism is an important aspect of every industry. Landscape irrigation is no different. Poorly designed or installed irrigation systems are seen as an inefficient use of our water supplies. This can lead to the outright ban of irrigation watering during periods of drought.*
>
> *"One of the best ways our industry can respond to this threat is by encouraging individuals to participate in continuing education, and demonstrating professional knowledge through certification. Numerous groups and associations offer these types of opportunities. The Irrigation Association is just one such organization. To succeed as an industry, we much constantly raise the bar of professionalism."*

Following are IA certification categories that are relevant to you as a landscape company owner. While not required, the IA offers courses to prepare you for the required exams:

- To become a Certified Golf Irrigation Auditor or a Certified Landscape Irrigation Auditor you'll need to attend a one-and-a-half-day course in either topic, and pass an exam. No prior experience is necessary.

- To become a Certified Irrigation Contractor you'll need at least three years of irrigation experience, or two years of experience and one year of related education. Then you must pass a written exam.

- To become a Certified Irrigation Designer you'll initially need at least one year of irrigation experience or education to apply. Then you must pass an exam before completing a total of three years' of related experience and two more exams.

For more information on the IA, you can call (703) 536-7080 or visit **www.irrigation.org**.

4. Planning Your Business

Having a game plan is crucial to the success of your landscape business. It can (and should) incorporate your own vision, and not be merely a cookie-cutter version of someone else's dreams. Developing a niche that showcases your aptitude and skills and allows you to provide a high-quality service that you can be proud of is a large part of the satisfaction that you will find through owning your own landscape company.

This chapter will launch you on your way to success. It covers your business options, how and why to draft a business plan, and how to determine your funding requirements. It goes over the start-up and operating expenses to expect, and where to go for financial help. The chapter ends with a round-up of legal matters from licensing to taxes.

4.1 Business Options

Many entrepreneurs claim that getting started is the hardest part of launching any new business. There's so much to do, so where do you start? Getting over the hump and moving yourself and your landscape business forward can be done by answering a few focused questions:

- What landscape services do I want to offer?

- What are my options for offering these services?

- Who are my customers and how do I find them?

This section will provide you with the information and resources that you'll need to respond to these questions, and provide you with the starting points you need to transition into landscaping with confidence.

4.1.1   Starting Out on Your Own

Starting out on your own in the landscaping business is what I generally recommend. It's by far the easiest and most economical way to get started. In this scenario you will perform lawncare and gardening duties, which may include:

- Lawnmowing

- Edging

- Fertilizing

- Aeration

- Verticutting

- Flower planting and gardening

- Light trimming and pruning

- Other duties as desired (e.g., fall clean-up, raking, etc.)

Here are the nuts and bolts of what you'll need to get a one-person landscape company set up, which will be covered in more detail later on in the guide:

- Choose and register a name for your company

- Buy a domain name and set up a company website

- Register your company as a sole proprietorship

- Get a business license if your city requires it

- Get a separate phone line just for your business

- Buy a lawnmower, a one-ton truck, and other equipment

- Get insurance coverage

- Promote your business

Help From The SBA

The Small Business Administration (SBA) is a valuable free federal program offering a wealth of resources to help you in all facets of starting your landscape business. The SBA provides free training and information on everything from finding start-up funds to writing a sound business plan and managing your company for success. In 2002, the SBA joined forces with My Own Business, Inc. to offer a free online entrepreneur course for small business owners. There is also a Spanish version of the course as well. Their website is located at **www.sba.gov**.

4.1.2   Buying a Company/Taking over a Route

Instead of beating the bushes looking for customers, it may seem easier to you to just buy an existing maintenance route from someone retiring or moving out of state. Besides putting pen to paper and figuring out if it makes financial sense, there are other important considerations.

> **TIP:**   Always bring in a lawyer for this type of transaction — it's worth a few hundred dollars, believe me!

First, before you make another move, find out how the customers viewed the former owner. This is very important! If most of them were unhappy with the service, this may not be the time for you to play Superman and rescue everyone from their plight. Instead of welcoming you with open arms, they just as likely may be skeptical and think that anyone associated with the former owner must be a scoundrel, too.

Even if they're just mildly dissatisfied, they may be looking for an opportunity to hire the next-door neighbor's landscape company, and view this as the time to act. Even a customer who was happy with the other guy's company may want to pick their own replacement. There's no guarantee they'll be loyal to you.

In my opinion, it's almost always better to start from scratch and get your own customers on your own terms. After all, you're a skilled professional! The exception is when you know firsthand that the previous owner had an excellent reputation and performed high-quality work. In this case, make sure he or she is willing to spend time with you in tow talking to each and every customer, in person, about his or her respect and support for you and the high-quality service you'll continue to provide.

If you're really serious about taking over a route, spend a couple days talking to the customers (by yourself unless you know they got great service before), and do everything you can to earn their trust and respect. Look at this as an opportunity to get hired by would-be customers in need of your services. Dress neatly and hand them business cards and a list of satisfied customers they can contact, perhaps from when you worked for someone else.

Another caution taking over a route is the financial end of things. Is the owner getting out of the business because they're broke? Did they undercharge for services? These are important things to know. The last thing you need is to lose money inheriting someone else's problems! It's almost impossible to raise the other guy's rate right off the bat and keep his or her customers.

Another reason to run for the hills is if you notice poor-quality work, such as thin lawns full of weeds and a generally unkempt appearance. Staying away from situations like these is your best bet.

4.1.3 Franchising

Franchising? Isn't that something for people who want to buy a hamburger joint or own a piece of a motel chain? You may not have even thought about it being a possibility in the green industry. But franchising is alive and well. There are several green industry franchisers out there serving residential and commercial markets. In addition, there are franchisers that exclusively serve niche markets in landscape irrigation and holiday decorating.

The five major lawn maintenance franchisers (Organicare, Lawn Doctor, NaturaLawn of America, Spring Green, and U.S. Lawns) require between $35,000 and $125,000 initially for franchise fees, including liquid capital of between $15,000 and $55,000 up front to qualify and about $8,000 working capital for startup expenses. Check with the franchisers listed below for current rates and stipulations.

The ins and outs are the same as in any other industry for the most part. You follow a prescribed course that's very carefully laid out for you. And, the franchise is definitely in this with you, wanting very much for you to succeed, so they'll do whatever they can to get you customers, help you out, and keep things afloat. You will usually pay a one-time franchising fee up front, and then a percentage of your annual sales after that.

If you decide to venture into franchising, be prepared for a pretty lengthy interview. Franchisors want to make sure you're a good fit and will be as good for them as they will be for you. A reputation is a two-way street. Many provide (and require) extensive training before you're on your own.

The biggest downside is that there's not a lot of wiggle room for your own ingenuity — you can't change course in midstream if you suddenly have a brainstorm, at least without getting approval at the corporate level. So, if you know the horticulture end in and out but aren't as talented at the business side of things, you might be a good candidate for franchising.

What do you get out of it? The legal right to offer landscape or irrigation services using a company's trademark and business systems. You gain instant respect due to name recognition if you pick a reputable franchise to team up with. Just make sure it's truly a good fit.

Shop around if this is the route you think you want to go. Make sure you're passionate about the services and products you'll be offering and that your background is well suited to the goals of the company.

The income you can earn franchising can be more, less, or about the same as you would on your own. It largely depends on the potential of the franchiser itself, the location of your particular market, and how well you're suited to this kind of profession. If it's the right fit for you, you can make an excellent income (into the six figures) after a few years.

- *Lawn Doctor*
  www.lawndoctorfranchise.com

- *NaturaLawn*
  www.nl-amer.com/lawn_care_franchise/
  lawn_care_franchise_opportunity.htm

- *NutriLawn*
  www.nutri-lawn.ca/recruiting/qualify_1.htm

- *Spring-Green*
  http://franchise.spring-green.com

- *U.S. Lawns Franchise Opportunities*
  www.uslawns.com/franchise_opp/default.asp

- *Weed Man*
  www.weedmancanada.com/franchise.html

- *EnviroMasters (Canada)*
  www.enviromasters.com/opportunities.shtml

4.2 Your Business Plan

I know. Just the name "business plan" can send chills down your spine and make your heart race, especially if you've decided to become a landscaper because of your love of being outdoors and dislike of an office setting. Resist the temptation to just wing it.

If you've never written one before, a crucial first part should be budgeting enough money to hire a financial expert or accountant to help you with the basic plan. Take it little by little, piece by piece. You will get through it, and might even enjoy it, although I can't say I've ever heard of anyone leaving a landscape career to become an accountant, and have seen the reverse many times.

Why have a business plan? The long and short of it is, it will keep your head above water. A major reason many businesses fail is because their owners didn't spend enough time planning. A business plan forces you to think in the long- as well as short-term. It molds your business by identifying goals and timetables.

A well thought-out plan not only helps guide you through running your business, but is necessary for applying for loans and getting financial backers or investors. Walking into your appointment with the loan officer at the local bank with a well laid-out plan can be very powerful. You can also use it for marketing your business to commercial accounts, potential equipment and supply creditors, and even potential business partners.

Here's what to include in your business plan. This section will expand on each of these points below:

- The services your landscape company will offer

- How you're going to reach potential customers

- The name of your company

- Skills and experience you have

- The structure and size of your company

- How much (if any) start-up funding you'll need

4.2.1   Analyzing the Market

Your Services

Make a list of what services you'd most like to offer each season as a landscape company owner. This is one reason why I stressed the importance of working for a year or two for someone else; you'll have a much better idea what you're really interested in doing and know what it entails.

Be as realistic as you can, but don't be afraid to be creative and do a little brainstorming. Potential lenders usually look favorably on good ideas, as long as they're pretty sure that any loan they grant can and will be repaid. Something too outlandish may not wash.

The Competition

Do some market research. This can be fun, because you learn a lot about how many competitors you have and what they're up to. Start by looking under "landscaping" or "lawn services" in your local Yellow Pages. Study the ads. What are your competitors offering? Who would you hire if you were in the market for a landscaper yourself?

Don't get discouraged and decide to throw your business plan out the window if it looks like the market is flooded. In landscaping, there's always room for another professional. It's a growing, rather than shrinking, industry.

Make sure your business plan includes specifics about the market research you've done and how and why your company will fit in the way you say it will. Don't even think about leaving this out. It shows a potential lender you've done your homework and aren't going to be another failed business in five years.

Looking at Your Research

Go back to the services you are thinking about offering. Modify them if necessary based on the data you've gathered about what the competition is doing. If your dream is to be a generalist and cover all aspects of residential gardening, for example, consider modifying how you'll promote yourself if you've discovered there's lots of competition.

Think about tapping into niche markets that aren't covered well in your area. If you're good at lighting and you've found out there's a huge need for it, or one that you can create, target that. If there's a need for a good deer-resistant landscape specialist in your area and you've got what it takes to provide this kind of service, go for it! Chapter 6 has more information on marketing your business.

How You'll Reach Customers

Describe in detail how you'll reach your customers. Include means such as flyers, mailers, door-to-door canvassing, a website, an ad in the Yellow Pages, and everything else you plan to do to attract not only a large number of potential clients, but the type you're catering to. If you're looking for upper-middle-class clients in a neighborhood of newly constructed homes, hone in on that particular market. Have a marketing plan specific to your needs and stick to it.

4.2.2   Naming Your Business

There are conflicting strategies about how to come up with a name that will get you noticed and bring in business. My advice is to keep it simple, yet as specific and personal as possible. For example, which sounds better to you:

- AAA Green Thumb Landscaping (using the old "start with multiple A's" trick to get listed in the phone book first!)

- Tom's Custom Lawncare

Many customers will let their fingers do some walking beyond the A's. Also, you'd be surprised how many people try to remember the name of a company written on a truck in front of a landscape they admired while driving by. The simpler or catchier the name, the better.

If you're in a niche market, make sure to include what services you specialize in. If Tom, in the above example, is also going to provide shrub care and general gardening services, he's chosen the wrong company name and will limit his sales base. If, on the other hand, he's going to specialize in only lawncare, he's got the perfect name.

Here's another example. Kathy is going to specialize in native plants. Her choice of names? "Kathy's Native Plant Services." Great! Doesn't that sound better than "Kathy's Landscape Service" for what she'll be doing? If you were a homeowner in the market for someone to plant and maintain a water-efficient native garden, I bet you'd call her.

A mistake I often see is a company name that can be misinterpreted if a potential customer just sees your truck driving around town and nothing more. An example is "Larry's Lighting." If Larry is specializing in outdoor landscape lighting, he's missing the boat by not specifying this in his company name.

By law, you'll need to make sure your business name is not already taken. You can check this out on the Internet or by personally going into the county recorder's office and having them do a search of the database. Once the name is yours, you'll have exclusive rights to it, although you'll need to renew it from time to time before it expires.

4.2.3 Your Own Qualifications

Write a convincing, but honest, resume. Make sure you include all pertinent education, skills, and experience you have. Don't be overly humble, but don't embellish things either.

Your resume is very important and often the first thing a potential lender will study. Having the most cleverly named business in the world filling a wide-open niche won't get that loan check in your hand if you can't convince a potential investor you have the background to run a company. Now you can see another really good reason to get that year or two of experience under your belt, can't you? If you don't do it on your own, your loan officer might insist on it.

If you have more education than experience, highlight that, along with a list of applied real-world classes you took that show you know the practical end and not just the scholastic side of things. If you have more experience than coursework, that should go on top.

List specific skills rather than just general statements. For instance, if you have training in designing and installing irrigation systems, include how you learned the trade and how long you've been doing it. If you have a certificate or license, be sure to include that, too.

If your experience is more general (which I think is best in most cases) you'll have several impressive skills you can include, such as developing irrigation, fertilization and integrated pest management schedules, as well as mowing lawns. Wording is important, too. Use terms that show you have a true knowledge of the profession.

4.2.4 Business Structure and Size

In your business plan you will describe whether your company will be a sole proprietorship, a partnership, or a corporation, as explained in the upcoming section on legal matters. This is easier if you're going to be a one-person company, and gets more complicated if you'll be hiring lots of employees.

I suggest that you don't appear to be too "pie in the sky" at first, but start reasonably small, with growth projections clearly laid out. If you plan on having an office manager and two or three employees in a few years, make sure you map this out, along with associated costs for physical space, added equipment, overhead, insurance, etc. Include projections from the day you open your company to two, five, ten and twenty years down the line. Back your guesstimates up with some hard facts based on your market research and reasonable growth plans.

This is where hiring an accountant for even just an hour or two before you put the finishing touches on your business plan comes in very handy. Save money by getting your thoughts about where you want to be two, five, ten and twenty years down the line on paper before sitting across from the accountant with the clock running.

4.2.5   Your Funding Requirements

Describe in detail any start-up funds you'll need and how you intend to acquire them. This is not only important for your own planning, but is also a necessity for applying for a loan.

You'll need to know what equipment you'll need and what it will cost (see section 5.1 for information), as well as all other expenses, overhead, insurance costs and contingency to cover any costs you haven't projected. The upcoming section on budgeting will also help you with these determinations.

Putting it all Together

Always include a page or two summarizing your plan, called an executive summary. Be concise and clear. Cover only the "bottom lines" you laid out in detail in the plan, focusing on your specific goals and how you'll accomplish them in the short, mid and long term. Include a sentence about your qualifications, and another couple about what you can supply financially and what you'll be asking a lender for.

Your completed business plan doesn't need to be printed on $2-a-sheet linen paper. It should be well written (use the spell-check function on your word processing program if spelling's not your thing), look professional, and be laid out attractively.

It's a good idea to run it by a close friend or family member who will give you an honest opinion about its tone and clarity. Avoid going to that warm and fuzzy friend who always tells you everything you say and do is perfect! While that kind of friend is great to have, in this case you really need a person who's not afraid to tell you what they really think.

4.3   Start-up Expenses

Service businesses like landscaping can be started for a minimal cost, since you don't have to have an office, factory, or retail space to work out of, or an inventory to purchase. In this section we'll look at some of the expenses specific to landscaping, as well as general expenses for any business. If your numbers are telling you that you'll need financial assistance, pay special attention to the section on financing options.

4.3.1   Expenses to Expect

When starting up a general landscape business, your two major expenses will be the following:

- Truck, at least a one-ton flatbed, good quality, used: $12,000+

- Other equipment and supplies, good quality, used: $3,000 to $4,000

You'll also have costs you'll need to cover that include your business license and other necessary permits, computer hardware and software, domain registration and website design, office supplies, and start-up advertising. You may need to prepay your annual insurance ($2,000 - $4,000).

You should budget enough in your start-up funding to cover your operating expenses for anywhere from three months to a year. This way you won't run into a cash shortage while you are waiting for clients to pay you. Once you are up and running, you'll need to factor in the following operating expenses.

- Vehicle depreciation, fuel and oil ($3,000+, depends on your mileage)

- Equipment rental (aerator, verticutter)

- Your wages

- Employee wages (if you hire anyone)

- Insurance

- Overhead (renting office space, utilities)

- Attorney and accountant fees

- Subscriptions to trade journals

- Association memberships

- Service club dues

TIP: Always add 10-15% for contingency funds to cover expenses you underestimated, which happens more than you think.

4.3.2   How Much You Will Need

You need to figure out the amount you'll need to ask the lending institution for after adding up the projected expenses and subtracting the amount you can invest yourself. A lender isn't going to sign over funds to you without some financial backing and reassurance from you that you're invested in the success of your company, too. Having this written up clearly and neatly shows you've given all this a lot of thought. It can have a very positive influence on a loan officer, who will size you up as someone who's organized and has a good chance of making a go of your dream.

You'll need to make some best-guess projections, working backward, regarding sales and how much income you'll need once you open up shop to stay in the game one, two, five, ten, and however many years down the line you want to keep your company going.

If your goal as stated in your business plan is to run your own show and never hire any employees, you obviously don't need to bring in as much income each year as if you had a crew of five.

When you're calculating your expected profit, it's a really good idea to know what the average is for your specific type of landscape work in your area. That's another very good reason to join trade associations and attend their functions. You'd be surprised how openly things like costs and rates are discussed among peers, especially if they don't view you as a toe-to-toe competitor because you work in another town or at least several miles away.

Even if your goal is to be the best landscaper in town, there's always going to be a cap on what the market will bear for your services. But, by all means, don't undersell yourself and put yourself in a position where you have to work 16-hour days because you bid too low and have to pay the price. There's a middle ground, and keeping your costs and expenses down is a good way to maximize your profit.

Put together monthly profit and loss (P and L) statements for at least a three-year period. This takes time, but maybe not as much as you think. If at all possible, get a good program and use a computer. Another way to do this is to sign up for an entry-level business class at a community college where this work could actually fulfill the requirements of an assignment and grant you access to a computer lab.

After you're finished, you might even want to sit down with whatever accountant you're going to use at tax time (always a good idea and usually well worth the money) for an hour with your sample P and L and business plan to make sure you're covering all the categories you need to — especially on the expense side.

Don't be surprised if no matter how you finagle the books, you're going to lose money at first. This is often the case. It just needs to be within reason for your potential earnings the next few years. If you decide to apply for a loan, being able to tell a potential lender that you've discussed this with your accountant and have five years of P and Ls projected will also boost your chances of getting that loan.

4.3.3   Sources of Funding

After you've done all your preparation and projections, you'll know whether you have enough start-up capital or if you need to get a loan. If you need a little help, you're well prepared at this point to make a good impression on potential investors. Where should you go? Here are some options.

SBA

Apply for a Small Business Association (SBA) guaranteed loan. If your landscape company will be operating in the United States, you can submit a loan application to a Small Business Association lender. If it's approved by the lender and the SBA, you're on your way. While payments are made directly to the lender, there are no application fees, points, or prepayment penalties, and payments can be customized to best fit the needs of your business. For more information, check out the SBA's website at **www.sba.gov**.

Home Equity

Apply for a home equity loan. This can work if you have enough equity in your house or another piece of property, and in a strong housing market. Interest rates vary, but at this writing are still relatively low, and offer tax advantages as well.

Personal Bank Loan

Apply for a personal loan from your credit union or bank. If you've been a loyal customer for several years and have good credit, you've got a good chance of being approved, especially if you're opening up a business account for your new company there, too.

If you're too new to an area to have built up a reputation with a local bank, you may still be able to obtain a loan. It's often advantageous to make an appointment with a small, local bank rather than a larger corporation. Shop around, since rates and payment schedules will vary.

Buy Equipment on Credit

Take advantage of equipment vendors offering credit (see section 5.1 on equipment). When you buy a vehicle or large piece of equipment such as a lawnmower, shop around for a reputable company that will let you charge the purchase, or a big chunk of it. This works well if you're sure you'll have enough accounts receivables to make the monthly payments.

Friends and Family

Get a loan from a relative or friend. This can work very well, or be a disaster. It's usually not the best idea, but you're in the best position to make this decision.

4.4   Legal Matters

Bill Baker, founder and president of William Baker & Associates, a successful southern California landscape company, offers this insight about the business of landscaping:

> "Owning and managing a landscape company is more about business than it is about landscaping. Many individuals who purchase or develop a landscape company have training and experience in some area of horticulture. While this is a helpful start, it is equally important to understand the several elements that constitute good business management practices, as well as the legal requirements, involved in successfully running a small business. The failure of a business can frequently be attributed to poor management systems and bad business decisions, rather than a lack of technical expertise."

Trust Bill. Make sure you get some solid business advice if you need it. Believe it or not, there are a few people out there who would rather be bean counters than tree planters!

4.4.1   Types of Business Structures

Once you decide to start your own landscape company, you need to decide how to structure your company. Whatever you do, don't choose to do nothing. You'll end up getting tangled up in legal woes at some point.

It's not as difficult or as expensive as you might think to get your company up and running legally. I suggest that you get some advice from a good accountant or an attorney if you're going in with another person or two and forming something other than a sole proprietorship. Each legal form of business ownership has its advantages and disadvantages, and getting a little professional advice is always a good idea.

Sole Proprietorship

This is the simplest and least expensive way to set up a small business. You solely and independently own your business and are responsible for all profits and debts. You're your own boss and get to make all the decisions. Also, your profits are taxed as personal income, which is often an advantage. The downside is the risk of personal liability. If your debts exceed your business assets, debtors can (and probably will) go after your personal assets. These include such things as your home, vehicles, bank accounts, and investments.

Partnership

In this arrangement, you and at least one partner own the landscape company, and agree to profit share. It's fairly easy to get set up, and your tax structure is the same as if you were the sole proprietor. Company profits and losses can be divided in any way you and your partners agree on.

Partnerships work well if the co-owners have compatible skills and agree on the company vision. If you choose this route, even if your partner is your best friend and you've known him or her since kindergarten, get everything in writing. This includes specific responsibilities of each partner; financial and equipment investments of each party; how profits, losses, and debts will be handled; how disputes will be resolved; your views on bringing future partners on board and what will happen if a partner leaves; and how assets will be divided if the business closes.

As with a sole proprietorship, a major disadvantage to a partnership is unlimited liability. In this case, individual partners are individually and jointly responsible for all debts and liabilities. This means that poor choices by one can financially devastate the other, so be wary of setting up this kind of business ownership.

Limited Partnership

In a limited partnership, there is at least one "general" partner who manages the business and one or more "limited" partners who generally stay out of the business end but contribute capital. Sound too good to be true? Here's the downside. The limited partners also legally share in the profits while the general partner is personally liable for all debts. This setup encourages investors since they can't lose more money than they originally put in if the business loses money or fails.

Corporation

A corporation has the benefit to its owners of being considered a separate, stand-alone entity. If there's a lawsuit, it is solely the corporation being sued, and you and your personal assets are protected. You are not personally responsible for debts, either.

Corporations often raise large amounts of business capital by selling shares (stock). The downside is that your corporation is taxed on two counts, because not only are you assessed taxes based on income, but also on outstanding shares of stocks.

Starting a corporation is not easy and it's expensive, costing several hundred to into the thousands of dollars since you'll need legal help drawing up your charter and taking care of other startup responsibilities. Corporations are strictly regulated by the government and require the filing of both state and federal reports. There is a loophole: forming an "S" corporation. This avoids double taxation (you're taxed as a partnership) but you have to meet certain requirements and there are other stipulations. Never enter into incorporation without first seeking the advice of an attorney specializing in this area.

Limited Liability Company (LLC)

This newer form of ownership is now available in most states. It offers the limited liability advantages of a corporation along with the tax advantages and management flexibility of a partnership. The downside is that it's more complicated to set up than a general partnership. A LLC is set up for a given length of time, which can be extended by members through a vote.

4.4.2 Taxes

Taxes are a fact of life, as they say. But, there's lots of free help to assist you in keeping everything straight. A good place to begin is with the Internal Revenue Service (IRS). They offer a Small Business Resource Guide interactive CD-ROM that is easy to follow and user-friendly. It is updated every year and covers any new tax laws that affect you as a small business owner. There are also lots of other materials, including a tax calendar for small businesses, which will help you meet those important deadlines. You can find all of these things at **www.irs.gov**.

You've probably heard the terms "fiscal year" and "calendar year" before. You have a choice whether to file your taxes by April 15th for the previous calendar year, as you do for your private returns, or pick another date. That becomes your fiscal year. The important thing to remember is that if you choose to file at another time during the year, you have to continue doing so and can't make a switch.

Most landscapers I know who own small companies that are operated as sole proprietorships choose to go with the calendar year approach, since they can file their personal and business taxes conveniently all at once. There are additional forms depending on whether you want to itemize equipment and depreciation schedules. It is a good idea to talk to a tax expert if you plan on doing any fancy filing. In any case, it's always smart to keep your business records completely separate from your personal ones, and definitely to use a separate checkbook and ledger.

When filing as a sole proprietorship without any employees, you do not need an Employee Information Number (EIN) and may use your social security number instead. You do need to keep receipts of all income received, as well as for business expenses you wish to deduct, such as business lunches and meetings and business-related travel.

Your business income and losses are reported on form 1040, Schedule C and self-employment tax on Schedule SE. If you have your business set up as a partnership, you must acquire an EIN and file income and losses on form 1065 and your partner's share on K-1. Of course, you have state tax responsibilities as well, and need to file a state income tax return.

Limited Liability Corporations and Limited Liability Partnerships are treated as a sole proprietorship or partnership by the IRS. If you form a corporation, consult a tax attorney for required forms. Few, if any, of you will likely choose to incorporate your small business, at least early on.

4.4.3   Licensing Requirements

Although you'll need to obtain a local business license, most states do not require landscapers to be licensed, especially those that specialize in the maintenance end of the profession. There are hundreds of landscape maintenance firms across North America that individually gross more than $500,000 annually, and plenty of room for many more.

However, I strongly recommend that you work toward gaining as many credentials as possible once you start your company. This can be accomplished over time. It's good not only for your professional growth, but also for gaining customers, who place a high value on these credentials.

Business License Requirements

You will need to get a business license from the city your company will be based out of. While you're at it, make sure there's no zoning restriction preventing you from operating your business out of your home.

You will also need to file a Fictitious Business Name Statement (don't you love that name?) for your company. This is also known as a "Doing Business As" (DBA). You can do this online or at your county recorder's office. This is to make sure the name you've chosen for your company isn't already taken or copyrighted, and it gives you rightful ownership.

You'll need to run an ad in a newspaper with general circulation in your county a few times over the course of about a month, to ensure that anyone who is interested has access to the true name and address of the business owner. Shop around. These ads can vary in price quite a lot and smaller papers offering this service often charge about half of what a mainstream paper might. By the way, you don't need to write the ad yourself; it's standard. You don't have to go through all this if you use your legal name for your company name or if you're filing a charter to become a corporation.

You will also need to obtain a seller's permit from the State Board of Equalization, to process incoming and outgoing taxes on goods and services. In Canada, you'll need to register with federal and provincial authorities in order to collect sales tax and the GST.

State Landscape Contractor Licensing

A contractor's license is generally not required for landscapers if you provide only general gardening and lawncare, and don't install hardware, apply pesticides, or prune trees taller than about 15 feet.

Many landscapers decide, at some point, to delve into the construction field, installing hardscapes such as decks, retaining walls, barbecues, gazebos, and patios in addition to continuing to offer maintenance services. While the vast majority of states do not require landscape builders to be licensed and/or registered contractors, some states, such as California and Arizona, do.

By definition, a landscape contractor installs plants and may install water features, irrigation systems, fences, decks, driveways, walkways, retaining walls and lighting for compensation. Some states define compensation as $500 or more per job, including plants and labor.

Regarding licensing, California is the strictest, requiring that all companies who charge $500 or more per site for any given service (even if it's merely planting hundreds of annual bedding plants) or prune a tree over 15 feet tall be licensed. Other states, such as North Carolina and Oregon, strongly urge landscapers to become licensed contractors, offer training and testing, and prosecute any self-labeled "licensed contractors," although neither require licensing for those advertising themselves as "landscapers" or "gardeners." California, Utah, Arizona, and Nevada offer reciprocity, which negates the need for a contractor from one state working in one of the other three to take that state's contractor exam.

Alternately, many states leave licensing and registration up to local jurisdictions. There is a state-by-state directory of contractor licensing boards at **www.contractors-license.org**. Contact them for specific requirements regarding becoming a licensed landscape contractor and any further requirements in any specialty area, such as electrical and/or plumbing work.

Usually, the company owner or a lead employee, but not both, are required to be licensed with the state contractors' board. Most states require between two and four years of experience and education before you're eligible to take the contractor exam. Licensing requirements can often be chiseled down if you have character references and valid insurance.

Some states offer open-book exams, and some closed. Here are some sample questions that are similar to those found on the California State License Board landscape contractor exam (a closed-book exam):

When is the best time to remove thatch buildup in cool-season lawn?
A. Mid to late winter
B. Mid to late summer
C. Mid to late spring
D. Mid to late fall (correct answer)

What effect does lime have when added to soil?
A. It increases the pH (correct answer)
B. It decreases the pH
C. It increases the potassium
D. It decreases the potassium

Irrigation Licensing

While some states or local jurisdictions require licensing for irrigation contractors, particularly those involved in plumbing and electrical work, many do not. If you are planning on doing much irrigation work, though, I strongly advise you to obtain specialty training in one of the four areas offered through the Irrigation Association, mentioned earlier. Obtaining this training will not only improve your expertise, but will also improve your competitive ability to gain valuable clients.

Pesticide Licensing

All states require that anyone applying pesticides be licensed. Most states now accept online coursework in addition to that obtained in a traditional classroom for completing continuing education requirements. Green Industry Education (**www.greenindustryeducation.com**) has compiled two very useful tools under their "LandsInfo" section: a list of each state's websites for obtaining information on pesticide licensing, and a list of states that allow online continuing education.

4.4.4   Insurance

Having insurance not only protects you, your company and any employees you have, but it's the law. I know it's easy to look at it as a waste of money and an unnecessary expense, but as soon as you need it and don't have it, you'll change your mind pretty quickly. I've heard some pretty horrible stories, and I'm sure you have too.

Laws vary from state to state, but the basics are generally the same. You'll often get the best rates from an agent not tied to one company. These are called independent agents.

Prices can vary for the same basic policy (except for board-set worker's compensation, as discussed below) so it's really wise to spend a half a day or so calling and asking around. Sometimes green industry trade associations link up with providers and will offer a significant discount if you join. Here's what you'll need.

Business Liability Insurance

This is for those mistakes that you never expect to happen, but sometimes do. Like a new employee unfamiliar with how the new truck works backing into a gas pump, or running over a prized three-wheeler sitting where it should be, right in the driveway! You just didn't see it.

Hopefully, no one's ever injured in these mishaps, but if they are, there's also coverage for personal injury and medical expenses. It covers all sorts of other things, too, like damage due to fire or water, and equipment theft.

Worker's Compensation Insurance

All states require this coverage. It pays for costs related to injuries sustained by your workforce. Rates are standard within a state and a category, so you might just as well buy it from the agent who offers you the best deal on business liability insurance.

Truck and Automobile

In addition to covering yourself, you'll need to buy group coverage for everyone driving your company vehicles. If your crew does any company-related work using their personal car or truck, you'll need to cover that too, or you could be held liable. Rates vary not only from company to company, but due to driving records. Depending on where your business is located, you might need a buy a permit for each vehicle you're going to use.

Bonds

Licensed landscape contractors and other specialists are almost always bonded. In essence, this is an insurance policy for the person you are performing work for. It covers losses if a project is abandoned and never completed, or for inferior quality of work.

This type of insurance isn't terribly expensive, unless you do a lot of large government contracting. Then the type of bond as well as the price go way up. As a landscape maintenance provider working in the residential sector, you usually do not need to be bonded.

5. Managing Your Landscape Company

Once you've got the basics in place, it's time to get ready to start offering your services. This chapter covers the tasks you'll need to do to run your business, such as purchasing the right equipment and tools, hiring and keeping great employees, and keeping an eye on your expenses and profit margin. It explains a number of different ways to charge your fees, and the factors to consider in setting them. Finally, it takes a look at how to keep your business going for years to come by being professional on the job.

5.1 Equipment and Tools

There's no question about it — when starting a landscape company you'll need to acquire the right tools and equipment to do a professional job, without going into too much debt. That can sound like quite a balancing act! Luckily, as mentioned earlier the start-up costs for operating a landscape company are not too steep.

So what will it cost you to purchase the minimum equipment you'll need to start a small landscape company specializing in lawncare, which is the least expensive end of the profession investment-wise? All in all, expect to spend a minimum of between $2,000 and $5,000 for equipment, supplies and clothing to get you started. Add the price tag of a good used one-ton flatbed truck, and you're good to go!

5.1.1   What You'll Need

Here are the basic tools you'll need to provide general residential light landscaping services:

Lawncare Tools

- ❏ Edgers

- ❏ Rotary (and possibly reel) lawnmower

- ❏ Fertilizer spreader

- ❏ Soaker hose

- ❏ Hose-end sprinklers

- ❏ Watering cans

Hand Tools

- ❏ Chainsaw

- ❏ Pruning saw

- ❏ Hedge trimmers

- ❏ Pruning shears (with holsters)

- ❏ Hoes

- ❏ Shovels

- ❏ Pole pruner

- ❏ Spades

Hauling and Cleanup Tools

- ❑ Brooms (push and utility)
- ❑ Large fork
- ❑ Cart
- ❑ Rakes (leaf and bow)
- ❑ Containers
- ❑ Wheelbarrow

Watering/Soil-Probing Tools

- ❑ Soil auger or corer
- ❑ Set of small straight-sided cans for irrigation can tests
- ❑ Irrigation nozzles, fittings and heads
- ❑ Several heavy-duty utility hoses (5/8")
- ❑ Pito tube

Miscellaneous Tools

- ❑ First aid kit
- ❑ Oil
- ❑ Heavy rope
- ❑ Rags
- ❑ High-quality basic building tools
- ❑ Sturdy industrial-strength ladder (at least 8 ft)
- ❑ Insect repellant
- ❑ Sunscreen
- ❑ Large water cooler (don't let yourself get dehydrated!)
- ❑ Tarps
- ❑ Measuring tape

Attire and Footwear

❑ Comfortable pants

❑ Raingear

❑ Few pairs sturdy shoes and boots

❑ Work shirts (ideally with your company name and logo)

❑ Hat

Remember that as your company grows and if you get your contractor's license, you'll need many more tools and implements for actual construction, grading and moving. Costs can easily double at that point. If you're licensed and will be applying pesticides, you'll need a sprayer (tank, backpack or both) and protective gear as required by law.

5.1.2 Buying Used

Instead of starting off with a brand-new $8,500 zero-turn mower, I suggest you buy a high-quality used one. Maybe it won't turn on a dime, but you'll get your company up and running with less of an upfront investment. There are solid deals out there on used equipment, especially when a new fancier model comes along that everyone wants.

Doug Jacobs of AA Equipment in Montclair, California, agrees that buying a high-quality used rotary mower is a better choice than a poor-quality new mower. Doug offers this advice.

> "A standard homeowner quality mower would get one started in business, but would not last in everyday use. The standard horsepower for 21" mowers is at least 5 to 6.75. It doesn't matter what color/manufacturer your equipment is; they all cut grass well.
>
> Ultimately it comes down to where you are purchasing your equipment. You could have the best piece of equipment out there, but if you do not have the parts and service to stand behind you, then what good is it if your equipment is in the shop? This is your bread and butter. Instead of looking at price, you should be asking questions like:
>
> • Does this dealer provide good financing?
>
> • If the equipment can't be repaired in a timely manner, will they provide a loaner?

- How long does it take to get parts?
- Is the dealership willing to listen to your needs and help you solve problems?"

There are more choices of lawnmowers today than ever before. Besides looking solely at the price of something as essential as a reliable rotary lawnmower, look at how much work the right equipment will save you in hours. In the Midwest where homeowners tend to have much larger backyards than western states, lawncare companies routinely buy large 72" riding mowers with 20 hp engines. In other parts of the country, where lawns tend to be much smaller, using a self-propelled walk-behind model can greatly reduce costs, sometimes by double or more.

Successful northeastern lawncare company owner Ken LaVoie of LaVoie's Landscape Management, Inc. in Winslow, Maine, agrees about the need for high-quality equipment, and knows firsthand how it can increase your profits. He says:

> "Get good equipment. Get the fastest equipment. Don't haggle price when buying the equipment you'll use most of the time, like mowers. Paying $2,000 more for a mower that gets an extra lawn a day done will pay for itself that very season."

Strike a balance. If your start-up costs are minimal, buy a good quality used industrial rotary mower at first, and use it the first season or two. If you budget right and include a reasonable profit margin in what you charge your clients, you should have more than enough money to upgrade to a more efficient one soon. If, on the other hand, you can afford it right away, consider buying a mower that will reduce mowing time right off the bat.

5.1.3   Where to Buy Equipment

A Local Dealer

It's a good idea to develop a solid business relationship with an equipment dealer you trust, and who carries both used and new equipment of several different makes and models.

There are many very good brands of landscape equipment out there, and you shouldn't necessarily narrow your choices to stay loyal to one brand. It's more important to buy quality equipment from someone you trust and who will offer high-quality service with a reasonably fast turnaround.

Make sure any dealer you're thinking about giving your business to cares as much about serving the needs of your small landscape company as much as he or she does about the needs of the "bigger guy" down the street. Many dealers actually want your business and value your loyalty, just as much as you do from your own customers. You can often get discounts over time, too.

When you're shopping around for a dealer, don't just pick one out of the phone book or online directory. Ask companies who have been around a while that are about the same size as yours where they buy their equipment. Since this isn't asking them to divulge any big insider secrets, they're usually pretty happy to help out.

Tradeshows

Tradeshows are an efficient way to look at lots of equipment from many manufacturers. They're usually free or inexpensive to get into, since exhibitors rent booths and display space that covers most of the show's expenses. Often, you can watch demonstrations and try out new products too. Some shows even offer fun events to draw big crowds like lawnmower races.

Once you get to the show, you can blend in with the group hanging out at the equipment dealer booths and listen to the banter between reps and potential customers, or strike up a conversation with the dealers. You can get a lot of insight this way.

Companies exhibiting at tradeshows tend to be on the up and up and send knowledgeable and reputable salespeople. After all, if they've had lots of complaints they don't exactly want to be a walking target for criticism all day long at a tradeshow!

There can be some pretty good deals at these shows. Often, manufacturers are there, and dealing with them directly can save you some money. Ask if any of their demonstration models are for sale, too.

Before you head over to the show, make sure you know what specifications you're looking for and the available options, so you won't get talked into buying more than you need. Even if you don't buy at the show, it's a great place to compare brands and prices and hobnob with colleagues — and get a few free hats and pens.

PLANET's website (**www.landcarenetwork.org/do/eventList**) has a list of upcoming industry events in the United States and Canada, including tradeshows. The Canadian Nursery Landscape Association (**www.canadanursery.com/Page.asp?PageID=122&ContentID=752**) lists tradeshows in Canada.

Other Equipment Sources

Buying equipment on the Internet is becoming more and more common. I think the best use of going online is to use it as a tool to do a lot of behind-the-scenes research on equipment makes and models before you talk to a local dealer or head to the tradeshow.

There are bargains to be found on the Internet, but check the warranty and make sure you can get whatever you buy serviced locally at a trusted facility. If you think you've found a terrific bargain online, you can also talk to a local dealer and ask them to match the price. Even if they still end up charging five or ten percent more, buying it locally and knowing you've got good service to back up your purchase might be a better choice in the long run. And, financial terms are often better. One thing's for sure. The next time you need those blades sharpened or replaced, you'll probably get better service for your loyalty.

What about equipment auctions? Auctions catering to the landscape industry are also becoming more and more common, thanks again to the Internet reaching across America. Used equipment and models that are being discontinued can be a solid deal. The same thing I mentioned earlier about weighing the disadvantage of not buying locally with the potential cost advantage holds true in this case, too.

Be sure to check out the *Grounds Maintenance Equipment Blue Book* values to make sure you're getting a good deal. This book costs $65, and can be ordered by calling 1 (800) 654-6776, or online from Price Digests at **www.pricedigests.com/other/groundsmaintequipbook.htm**.

5.1.4   Buying or Leasing

Okay, you've picked out your "toy." Now, how are you going to pay for it? Many manufacturers and dealers will finance your purchase, although, just like any other creditor, some deals are better than others, and rates are directly linked to the economic market at the time of purchase.

If you do decide to lease, shop around and get the best deal you can find. Interest rates can vary a lot, and are usually higher than rates charged for a new piece of equipment. Compare the best fixed rate you can get from a dealer with the rate you would pay using your personal credit card. Usually, the dealer's rate comes out ahead.

Another option many dealers offer is one where you make a relatively small down-payment at the time of purchase, and pay off the purchase balance over six months or even a year with no interest or fees tacked on. This is a great way to go and will save you money as long as you're sure you can pay it off in time! Many landscape company owners routinely choose this route even if they are in a position to make a heftier down-payment or even write a check for the full amount right there at the dealership.

Why? They'd rather earn interest on the money (even a business checking account with a large enough average balance will generate a percent or two), and are covered if any problems arise later on regarding use or warranty of the equipment. Basically, they're holding a few cards close to their chest if there's trouble.

Avoiding too high of a percentage of debt is important for the overall success of your company. Bill Baker, Founder and President of William Baker & Associates who has purchased many pieces of equipment over the years as a highly successful green industry business owner, knows this. He shares this advice:

> "Try to avoid investing in equipment until you have the customers or contracts to make the investment profitable. As with all businesses, a landscape company cannot operate without a steady cash flow. Do everything possible not to tie up cash you may need for daily operations. Be cautious about purchasing specialty equipment that has only

a periodic or seasonal use — e.g., aerifiers, stump grinders, lift trucks, and high-pressure sprayers. Rent this kind of equipment until you are sure that owning it means more than storing it at your facility."

Leasing equipment like aerifiers and verticutters that you'll use seasonally and don't need year around is almost always preferred over buying them. Leasing lawnmowers, on the other hand, can be a good or a bad deal. It's usually best to buy one if you can.

5.2 Hiring Staff

A landscape company can certainly be a one-person business, but often, over time, there is just too much for one person to handle. This section looks at evaluating your employment needs; employee issues such as keeping employees happy, reducing turnover, and dealing with personnel conflicts; and how to deal with safety issues on the job.

5.2.1 Evaluate Your Needs

Most landscape company owners find that while they're just starting out, it's preferable to keep their operation small and not hire any employees. In many cases, starting out as a one-person company and investing capital wisely on a good used truck, mower and some tools rather than employees is the best way to go. This gives you a chance to bring in some profits the first year to help defray the costs of buying a piece or two of other needed equipment the second year, and hiring a helper or two for you and possibly some part-time office help.

This, of course, depends a lot on your savings. If you've been successful saving money for a few years and have a pretty large nest egg going into your first year as a landscape company owner, you have more choices. You might want to hire a little help right away, and get a better mower and/or truck. Everyone's situation is a little different.

Whatever you decide, don't overextend yourself and go too far into debt. This can happen by buying too much equipment before you really need it, or hiring too many employees. Follow your business plan, and if you find your projections to be off quite a bit, make adjustments as soon as you can.

You may decide to hire a couple full-time entry-level employees in a year or two after you've built up your client base. Spend as much time as you can training them in both horticulture and people skills. Also, work closely with a trusted licensed contractor who can get you quality clients and to whom you can refer your customers when the skills, experience and licensing to get the job done are beyond your own. Remember that any contractors you subcontract need to have full workers compensation and general liability insurance.

What about some office help? About half the landscapers starting out choose to hire a part-time person, and half don't. A few actually sweet talk a significant other into helping out for free. If you and a family member mutually agree it's a family affair and decide to work together, I suggest you put them on the payroll just like you would anyone else.

Don't look at it like money coming out of your household's coffers. Look at it as a business expense and remember that salaries and a reasonable profit are included in each and every job and service you offer. This includes paying Mom or your husband or wife what you'd pay anyone else doing the same job. They should even get raises like you and the rest of the crew.

You're probably getting pretty worried reading this about how you're ever going to deal with payroll, taxes and keeping up with laws that seem to be constantly changing. One of the modern miracles of today's high-tech society are companies called Payroll Service Providers (PSP). Yes, it's as good as it sounds. Someone else can take care of paying your employees and filing payroll taxes on time, all for a very reasonable fee. It gets better. Many also take care of pre-employment screening and insurance and retirement plans. This is why a number of landscapers with no employees use them, too. There are many PSPs to choose from. They're listed in the phone directory and you can also pull up a number of them on the Internet using a keyword search.

It is definitely a good idea to budget a few hours for professional services from a good lawyer and accountant, especially to get the company started and help project income and expenses for the first few years. Investing $400 to $500 on these services can pay for itself the first year many times over.

What about hiring your own landscape designer? This may or may not be the best idea for your company. That's where your long-range business plan comes in. If you find that hiring an in-house designer fits best with your business plan and you know you could get more work in your geographical area with this arrangement, it may be the best option.

Expenses of hiring a designer can often be totally or mostly defrayed by service fees absorbed by your customers. The obvious advantage to you is that you two are truly a team, and the designer will know what your expertise and limitations are and will only design what you have the skills to build.

Having an in-house partner like this can save confusion and misunderstandings down the road. An advantage for customers is the one-stop shopping approach and the fact that there are fewer cooks in the kitchen, so to speak. Homeowners often prefer hiring one company to take care of an entire project, and are sometimes confused by where jobs of landscape designers, contractors and landscape maintenance personnel begin and end.

If you do decide to hire a designer, hiring the right person is extremely important for this arrangement to work well. Spend time checking out their work, talk to their references, and only hire a designer who shares your vision and sees eye to eye with you on the type and scope of design work that your company can do in a professional and timely way.

5.2.2   Keeping Employees Happy

Tom Heaviland, President of Heaviland Enterprises, Inc., a San Diego County, California commercial landscape management firm, says he owes his company's success to developing positive working relationships with employees, whom he treats with the utmost respect. He says:

> "We feel if we take care of our employees by providing them with the resources to succeed, they will, in turn, take care of our clients. I've come to realize that as a company, we are only as strong as those guys out in the field doing the work. So it makes sense to invest in developing them, personally and professionally. Great customer service starts with your internal customers first. Just look at companies like Southwest Airlines and Starbucks — great role models!"

Tactics such as the following are used by successful landscape company owners to inspire employees and make them want to come to work as much as you do.

Provide Decent Pay and Benefits

It's costly to train new employees over and over again, and keeping good ones should be a priority. Pay always has been, and always will be, a key motivator.

Paying a beginning laborer $8.50 an hour rather than $8.25 (for example) is one of the best methods out there to attract and keep good employees who will stick with you and want to learn the ins and outs of the business. Studies have shown that beginning laborers will sometimes leave one job for another for as little as a ten or twenty cent an hour pay increase.

Again, just make sure you build these costs of doing business into your cash flow projections. Hard work really does deserve financial recognition. And since you're the boss, you don't have to worry about a particularly hard-working employee trying to steal your job away, either!

Employee Benefits

Should you offer employee benefits? It's an added cost of doing business, but my own opinion is yes, you should definitely consider it. Besides knowing you're providing a very valued service, you'll be able to recruit and retain a steadier, more loyal workforce and the return on your dollar is pretty good.

More and more green industry associations are offering group plans by teaming up with providers. An example is Texas Mutual Insurance Company, who has had an enthusiastic response from green industry businesses to their group workers' compensation insurance. Texas Green Industry, a purchasing group, provides their members with workers' compensation coverage, and any Texas insurance agent can place a qualifying client into an open program group.

Another innovative program is offered by Bissett Nurseries in New York through Loyd Keith Friedlander Limited to landscapers and nurseries they service. They offer every type of insurance imaginable including liability, auto, professional errors and omissions, workers' compensation and disability, life insurance and many others. They even have an insurance desk set up at their nursery!

When you're choosing which green industry associations to belong to, check with your top picks about group insurance benefit plans you can take advantage of by joining. This can save you hundreds of dollars a year, depending on how many employees you have.

Other employee benefits are things like company picnics, trips to tradeshows and association meetings and activities, fresh hot coffee and sodas, and donuts every Friday morning. I consider these benefits rather than incentives (see section on incentives below) because they're not based on the performance, per se, of your workforce. You offer them to everyone and no one "earns them" over anybody else.

These "warm fuzzies" mean a lot to most employees, often more than you think. Again, when kept in reason, they're a great way to keep your crew happy and productive without breaking the bank.

Provide a Supportive Workplace

When your employees come to work, they want to be able to know they can go to someone for help and guidance for all kinds of work-related issues. Many studies have shown that executives actually suffer less job stress than their workforce because they're in control. They don't feel removed from decisions and know they can change something that's not working. An employee can feel pretty helpless when they've been dropped off on a jobsite without enough training to do the job right, let alone answer any questions the client might have about anything else that might come up.

Make sure you allocated plenty of time to train your employees, and the earlier, the better. This should be done the first few days or weeks they're on the job. Employee orientations that cover things like standard procedures for reporting and dealing with everything from problems on the site to mechanical failures, or flat tires are crucial.

If at all possible, draft an employee manual. It doesn't need to be long and look like something that Bill Gates or Donald Trump would come up with, but it should include things like who to go to for help filling out paperwork, what to do in the case of an accident, how to report work hours, when everyone will be paid, who to call when an employee is sick, how and when employees are considered for raises, and, of course, procedural information on what to do on the job site from a horticulture standpoint.

Having job descriptions for each position in your company is also important. You'd be surprised how often there just aren't any. That's when some real on-the-job confusion and disillusionment can set it. "Oops! I didn't know I was supposed to do that!" Not having a job description is worse than hearing an employee tell you they didn't do a task because "it's not in my job description." At least they're reading it!

New employees are often afraid to speak up about things they don't understand, believing that it will make them look stupid to their boss and everyone else who's been there longer (whom they're trying to impress). The more you can actively listen as well as explain things clearly, yet respectfully, the better.

Try to put yourself in their shoes. Think about what you'd want to know if it was your first day, week, or even month, on that job. Ask for their ideas, too, especially as time goes on. Just because they don't volunteer any at first doesn't mean they don't have plenty!

Never underestimate the intelligence, creativity and overall value each and every one of your employees brings to your company. Some beginning laborers have great mechanical skills. Take advantage of talents they bring on board. It's mutually beneficial to you and to them. They feel respected and will want to work even harder, and your company will "work smarter."

Offer Incentives

Incentives are usually rewards given to individual employees (or the team as a group) when production targets are met, or sales are increased. There's nothing like increasing productivity by spreading around the rewards.

However, there's also a fine line between turning employees trying to get bonuses into vultures and relying on them to help bring in business. A good employee handbook should spell out exactly what incentive plans are available, and how to professionally and diplomatically go about getting new customers and suggesting new services to loyal customers.

Let's say that your business plan calls for providing specialty services to ten additional customers in three different residential neighborhoods spread all over town over the course of three years. (This example might be lean in growing urban neighborhoods, or a little optimistic in tighter markets).

Your employees, who spend most of their time on job sites, can be your best recruits. They're outside, working in view of neighbors, and have more contact with your residential clients than you probably do.

Supply employees with plenty of company pamphlets describing your services (or at least a one-page company description), and business cards. Offer them a moderate on-the-spot bonus for each new service account they get, as well as a percentage of the profit when the job actually takes place. Be sure to build this into your fee structure or else your company will lose money.

To make this work, you're going to need employees with good communication skills as well as good horticulture skills. If your workforce does not have a mastery of the English or the native language of the client base, it's better for you to schedule some of your own time to canvass neighborhoods. Plan on visiting each job site personally every couple weeks to touch base with your clients and see how things are going. (Actually, this is a good idea whether you're trying to drum up more business or not!)

Another effective incentive plan is to have your employees talk directly to your residential customers about providing additional services for them while they're onsite performing routine maintenance duties. For example, offer bedding plant selection, installation and maintenance for a fixed price. Have your employees keep photo albums in their truck of similar work you've done. There is a relatively high profit margin on these services.

> **TIP:** Unless you or one of your employees is a licensed landscape contractor, be careful here. In some states, if a job exceeds $500 in installation and related services, you can be fined.

Other successful employee incentive programs include something like a paid afternoon off every other month for perfect attendance. "Employee of the month" programs can work if there's clearly a key employee who deserves this recognition, but if you've got two equally qualified employees and you picked one by the flip of a coin, it can create a lot of hard feelings. Sometimes the brunt of this is between the employees themselves, who spend more hours working side-by-side every week than they do with their families.

Every time you're honoring one person, you risk demoralizing other really good workers. There's nothing wrong with doling out due appreciation, but keeping it on a level playing field where everyone can earn it as long as they put out equal amounts of hard work (like drumming up business) seems to work best.

5.2.3   Dealing with Personnel Issues

Even if you're the best boss who ever walked the face of the planet and you've got the finest employee handbook ever written, you will, at some point, have personnel issues and problems to deal with.

Besides being a horticulturist, I've also served in enough administrative roles to know that personnel issues can eat up more time than just about anything else. Things like job duty issues can largely be kept at bay by having clearly spelled out job descriptions for everyone as we talked about before, but other things like personality conflicts can have more to do with human nature than anything else.

They will happen. That's the first thing, and a very important thing, you should know. If you think things will run squeaky clean and everything will be smooth sailing, you're setting yourself up for disappointment. A little realism mixed in with some healthy optimism that these things can be worked out is a good way to proceed!

Personnel issues can generally be grouped into three main categories, which we'll deal with in this section:

- Gripes about job conditions

- Conflicts with each other

- Conflicts with your customers

Gripes about Job Conditions

You can often sense that something is just not right by the way an employee looks at you, changes their demeanor, avoids you, shows up late, leaves early, etc. Whenever a disgruntled (evenly mildly) employee comes to you with a concern or complaint, never blow them off or dismiss their stance as petty or unimportant. Look them in the eye and really listen. It's a good idea to take notes, too.

An ounce of prevention is great too, which is why the employee handbook idea where issues such as employee pay, raises, time off and general working conditions are spelled out is so important. Many studies report that between 60 to 85% of employee gripes have to do with these very issues.

One way to avoid these from happening in the first place is to make sure any employee you hire knows what pay rate they're starting out at, terms and conditions of any probation period, what constitutes overtime from a legal definition (not your own), grounds for discipline and dismissal, and exactly what their job responsibilities are.

Ask your potential employees if they have any questions. Give them some time to think about accepting the job so they won't feel pressured to say yes to something they either don't really want or don't fully understand. It's unlikely that you'll ever lose a key employee by giving them this "think through it" time.

When conflicts occur, remember that it's not nearly as important who is officially right as it is to get the conflict out in the open and resolved. Don't turn every issue into a power struggle.

In some cases, the issue at hand will technically be the fault of the employee, while other times, it will be your fault. Mistakes do happen, and most misunderstandings don't start out as malicious attempts to undermine or discredit someone. But, they can sure turn out to look like that if things aren't taken care of. Problems tend to grow over time, and not disappear.

Try to do everything you can to get the problem resolved. If you need time to check some records to find out if there's paperwork to back up what your employee is telling you (they logged more hours than they were paid for, left you a note in your inbox about going to a doctor's appointment the next day, etc.), tell them that this is a serious concern to you and you'll get back to them. Set a time and a place to do this. Thank them for bringing whatever the matter was to your attention. And make sure you follow through. If you find out they're right, apologize right away and correct the error.

Of course, sometimes you're right and they erred. Maybe one particular employee routinely just doesn't get the job done. They do poor quality work (a huge concern in this industry), are rude to your customers, and complain to everyone about nothing most of the time. (In this case, assume that someone with that kind of attitude might also sue you.)

Look at the glass half-empty at this point and take action. Expect the worst. Sometimes, you just have to admit you made a mistake hiring someone and need to let them go. Lawsuits are something you want to try to avoid. They can drain your resources and put a real damper on everyone else's spirit. This is why I strongly suggest you have an attorney provide a template for writing up the section of your employee handbook dealing with discipline and grounds for firing. Follow it to a T.

Some companies have actual complaint forms that document every supposed offense. This can come off as a bit militaristic for some, but does have its advantages when it comes to what's on the record, especially if it ever ends up in court.

Conflicts with Each Other

Sometimes you'll have an issue with employees who just don't get along. Often, one isn't right and the other wrong all the time, it's just purely and simply a personality conflict. Sometimes personalities just don't mesh well, regardless of what a well-intentioned boss tries to do about it.

An obvious solution is to try to avoid it happening in the first place, just like with all the other employee issues we've been talking about. A good way to do this is to let your employees have a say in the hiring process. This works very well, especially with a relatively small company. You probably wouldn't want 15 or 20 employees holding an interviewee hostage for a couple hours asking them questions and intimidating them, but that's probably not the size of your company, at least for now.

Have any current employees that will be working much of the time with the new person involved at some level. Think about inviting potential teammates to participate in the actual interview for fifteen or twenty minutes. Let them come up with and ask a few questions about the person's skills and background pertaining to the job they'll be doing together. Look them over ahead of time to make sure they're not stuff that could get you in legal trouble.

It's amazing how well this can work. Most employees won't have it any other way after seeing the value in this. You can get feedback from your employees about how they think it all went. Pay close attention to what they tell you! Another good way to avoid personality conflicts and on-the-job squabbles is to ask current employees for referrals.

Conflicts with Your Customers

The other type of conflict deals with customer relations, and how your employees communicate with your clients. Hiring employees with good interpersonal skills is as important as their horticultural training.

You can have the most skilled lawn technician in the world on your crew, but if his or her communication skills and ability to get along with your clients aren't just as polished, you'll lose more ground than you'll gain. Your employees are the face of your company. It's better to remain on your own if you have to until you find a congenial employee who gets along with people.

Sometimes the problem doesn't lie with your crew, but with a customer who's just plain off base. This can be a very tricky issue. If you value this client, you have to do something to take care of the situation. Sometimes, a loyal employee gets on the receiving end of a tirade from a customer just waiting for a target to come along. It could be anybody. Your employee was just in the wrong place at the wrong time.

If you did a good job teaching your crew how to deal with these situations, you probably won't have nearly as much fallout. Letting your crew know that they should keep in mind that customers have bad days just like everyone else and may take it out on them prepares them for this kind of situation when it does happen.

Other times, there is anything from a minor to a serious issue between an employee and a customer that is due to a mistake made by an employee. An example might be a new, inexperienced crew member spreading fertilizer unevenly, leading to streaks in a week or two, or weeds taking over a flowerbed that is supposed to be tended.

Hopefully, what you're thinking is that those problems can pretty easily be avoided. Bingo! Good horticulture training is so important. Spend several days with new employees until they know exactly how to do every procedure and when to do them.

Talk to them about typical problems that can occur. And don't ever put the least experienced employee behind the fertilizer spreader full of urea. Make sure they get the hang of things with a slow-release product first. As far as the flowerbed, train your crew to stay on top of weeds, and explain how much easier they are to either hand pull or hoe when they're young. These are, of course, just a few examples.

With that said, what happens when there's a mistake, regardless of how carefully you've trained your crew? The first thing for them to do is let you (or a designated lead person) know about the problem right away.

Make sure your employees know that you don't expect things to go perfectly all the time, but the key is to get in touch with you or a designated lead person immediately when something goes wrong. Keep a cell phone with your crew and keep yours on. If you can't afford this, invest in a beeper. After you've assessed the situation, you'll know whether this rates a 2 or an 8 on a 1-10 scale, and how to deal with it.

Making sure your employees treat your customers courteously and with respect is vital. They should be patient and listen to every word a customer tells them, even when they've heard the same story a thousand times before. Occasionally you'll get an overly chatty customer, or one that's plain loony. Then the rules change somewhat and your crew should remain respectful, but stick to the job as much as possible.

Letting Someone Go

In some cases, it might become clear that an employee just isn't the right person for the job. They're nice enough, polite to clients, and really try hard, but just aren't developing the skills required in the horticulture field. While you can try to work with them and get them more training, sometimes it's just not in anyone's best interest. I strongly suggest you hire all your employees on a probationary basis. The situation I just described is actually pretty routine, and sometimes just isn't caught during the interview process.

Have a meeting with them and tell them you value their dedication and hard work, but their skills just aren't a good fit with your company. If you've offered no firm commitment after a "soft" six-month period and this kind of employee turns on you threatening a lawsuit, the law will be on your side. Otherwise, you need a lot of substantiation for why you're letting an employee go. The line can be fuzzy if they come to work on time, everyone likes them and there haven't been any big mishaps.

If at all possible, try to line up another job for a person mismatched with your company, or at least give them some leads. Maybe they've got terrific mechanical or electrical skills and really belong alongside a contractor or irrigation specialist. Of course, if they have severe attitude problems that are the major cause for their dismissal, then you'd be doing your industry a disservice by trying to pass them off on someone else just to get them out of your hair.

5.2.4   Staff Safety

Preventing accidents is obviously very important, and there can be serious ones in the landscape profession. If you stick to lawncare and general gardening and don't prune large trees or apply pesticides (both of which require licensing) you greatly reduce the risk of yourself or your employees being injured or developing work-related health problems.

That said, anytime employees operate or are around machinery like mowers, edgers, blowers, etc., accidents can happen. Spend lots of time showing your employees what it means to be safe on the job rather than just telling them. Go over every practice in detail, and provide training in Spanish if you need to. Back up all training with written information pertaining to safe practices on the job with emergency phone numbers, and forms in your employee handbook.

While the U.S. Occupational Safety and Health Administration (OSHA) is sometimes thought of as the federal program that makes sure you have politically correct bathrooms for your crew, they perform much more important roles in the workplace than that.

They are in charge of making sure that you and your crew follow strict health and safety guidelines on the job. They are a respected organization and provide excellent training and education. In fact, since OSHA was formed in 1971, workplace fatalities have been reduced by more than 60 percent, and work-related illness and injury by 40 percent.

You can learn more about OSHA programs, requirements, and education pertaining to small businesses by visiting their website. They also have many helpful publications available. Specific areas of interest that affect the landscape profession are:

- Preventing and treating heat stress and dehydration

- Safe use and handling of landscape machinery and tools

- Proper lifting to prevent back injuries

- Safe use and storage of pesticides and fertilizers

- Prevention of insect bites, stings and toxins from plants

- Hearing and eye protection on the job

- Responding to an emergency

Information can be downloaded from the website, or ordered from:

- *U.S. Department of Labor/OSHA*
  Address: OSHA Publications Office
                  200 Constitution Ave., NW
                  Room N3101
                  Washington, D.C. 20210
  Phone: (202) 693-1888
  Website: **www.osha.gov**

5.3 Budgeting for Success

If I had to guess, I'd say that budgeting just may be the least exciting part of the book for you. I'll try to do my part by making sure to use as many relevant examples to the landscape profession as I can, and I'll make it as concise as possible. You do your part and bear with me.

The bottom line is that pricing your services too low can close down your business faster than just about any other mistake. And working longer days to try to make up for mistakes won't get you out of the hole, either, if your costs exceed your income. In fact, it will only make things worse.

Why does this happen so much then? It's certainly not because landscapers don't want to earn a decent income, or that they're not motivated or bright enough to figure it out. I think it's the same reason most small business people don't budget like they should. The whole language of accounting is often presented in a very theoretical way, and so it's hard to figure out just how it relates to running your specific business.

Instead of someone just giving you a straight answer like, "Running a successful landscape business requires you to charge $40 an hour to make a profit of $10,000 a year and pay you a salary of $35,000," which is what all of you really want to hear, you get referred to five pages of balance sheets you're supposed to fill in. You can't get around it. You do need to plug a few numbers in. But it doesn't have to be as bad as you think.

Lawncare companies generally charge residential customers between $25 and $50 an hour, depending on what part of the country they're in. The bottom line is to make sure you cover your expenses (direct and indirect) and make a reasonable profit. Here's how.

5.3.1 Your Expenses

There are many ways to list your expenses, but the key is to make sure they're all accounted for. Start with all the expenses that remain constant each month. We'll call them fixed expenses. The amount you need to pay is standard.

ITEM	MONTHLY COST	ANNUAL COST
Advertising	$25.00	$300.00
Association Dues	$20.00	$240.00
Certification/Licensing	$15.00	$180.00
Insurance	$200.00	$2,400.00
Salaries/Benefits	$2,800.00	$33,600.00
Telephones	$70.00	$840.00
Vehicle Payment	$200.00	$2,400.00
TOTAL	**$3,330.00**	**$39,960.00**

Next, list all the expenses you need to pay over the course of the year. These are called variable expenses because they vary in amount from month to month. Including a 10 percent contingency in your grand total will help you pay for unexpected expenses such as goof-ups and expenses due to underbidding time, materials, or both.

ITEM	AVERAGE MONTHLY COST	ANNUAL COST
Clothing/Boots/Shoes	$20.00	$240.00
Computer (website, email, software)	$40.00	$480.00
Education (books, seminars, subscriptions)	$20.00	$240.00
* Equipment Rental	$50.00	$600.00
Gasoline and Oil	$200.00	$2,400.00
Office Supplies/Postage	$25.00	$300.00
* Landscape Supplies/Materials	$70.00	$840.00
Tools	$25.00	$300.00
Travel (personal car used for meetings)	$25.00	$300.00
Vehicle Expense/Repair	$40.00	$480.00
Professional Services (attorney, accountant)	$40.00	$480.00
TOTAL	$555.00	$6,660.00

*For routine maintenance work.
Specialty jobs (planting flowerbeds, etc.) are charged by the job.

EXPENSES — GRAND TOTAL	MONTHLY COST	ANNUAL COST
Fixed Expenses + Variable Expenses	$3,885.00	$46,620.00
+ 10% Contingency	$4,274.00	$51,282.00

This means that your landscape company will need to bring in $51,282 a year simply to cover expenses. Anything you make above and beyond that is called profit, and is usually calculated as a percentage.

Set your pricing structure based on how much money over the course of the year it takes to pay for all your direct and indirect expenses, and what level of profit you want to make. It is really easy to overlook some of these important costs. This is cited by many landscapers as a number-one way to start digging your grave. Even during the off-season, you're going to need to cover some year-round expenses.

Make sure that every single expense it takes to run your business is included in charges passed on to your client base. Otherwise, these costs are coming out of your own pocket or any profit you're trying to build up.

5.3.2   Making a Profit

How much should you charge per hour? Let's plug the above figures in and see. In the above example, you'd need to charge at least $37.82 an hour just to cover expenses. If you bump that up to $45 an hour, you stand to make $9,736.08 in annual profit. Note that this is not your salary — that is calculated in your expenses. This is money that can reinvested back into the growth and sustainability of your business.

I calculated the figures based on you working 226 days a year, which gives you a two- week vacation and billing hours based on a six-hour day. A very common mistake is to base billing hours on an eight-hour day. This is fine if you can swing it. But, you not only have driving time, but also time needed for clean up and equipment maintenance.

Here's another caution. If, for example, you find that you've done better than you expected getting lots of word-of-mouth jobs and are able to cut down a bit on some ad costs you were planning on, think carefully before you decide to pass along these "savings" to your customers with a reduction in your fees. It could be that next year things change and you'll need to recoup these expenses, so store it along with your other profit in an interest-earning account, and give yourself a pat on the back.

Electronic Help

If you are still struggling with these figures, for a few hundred dollars of very well spent money, you can download any number of excellent business software programs specifically designed to fit the needs of the landscape industry, often written by landscapers themselves. Programs vary widely by services offered and costs, ranging from around $75 for basic to more than $3,000 for more involved operations in which you can add more than 20,000 customer accounts.

You just plug in your annual expenses and the amount of profit and salary you're aiming for, sit back, and let a sophisticated program spit out the results. Just like that. I'm really sold on these programs and think they're well worth the annual investment. You'll probably recoup the expense in just a couple months, because you'll be making a profit from the get-go.

- *Groundskeeper Pro and Groundskeeper Lite*
  Phone: 1 (800) 586-4683
  Website: **www.adkad.com**

- *Gopher Billing and Support Software*
  Phone: 1 (888) 606-5150
  Website: **www.gophersoftware.com**

- *Real Green Systems, Inc.*
  Phone: 1 (800) 422-7478
  Website: **www.realgreen.com**

- *CompuScapes*
  Phone: 1 (800) 350-3534
  Website: **www.compuscapes.com**

- *Active Applications: UDS Green Industry Software*
  Phone: 1 (800) 626-7247 (U.S. and Canada)
  Website: **www.udsgis.com**

Ways to Tweak Your Numbers

If your landscape company is in a region that just won't bring in that kind of money, you're going to have to find a way to reduce expenses. If you're living in a state with a lower cost of living, then costs for running your business are less, too. It all tends to average out.

Don't forget that there are many specialty services you can offer during the season that will increase your company earnings pretty substantially. They have higher profit margins than straight landscape maintenance work. Whenever you can, take advantage of these opportunities. These include:

- Aerification

- Verticutting (thatch control)

- Planting annuals and perennials

Remember that there is money to be made in supplying plants to customers. You can often make twice what you paid for them at the wholesaler and still match what your clients would have had to pay on the retail side. These specialty jobs are charged by the job rather than by the hour. Many landscapers easily clear $2,000 to $5,000 during the season by offering these services.

For all you landscape company owners living in Minnesota, North Dakota and Maine, I haven't forgotten that you've got frozen ground several months a year. We talked about off-season opportunities in section 2.6, so take advantage of these. Unless you're in the sunbelt, you're going to need to do something besides landscaping to bring in at least $38 an hour six hours a day, or $228 a day!

5.3.3   Growing Your Business

When you hire employees, the picture changes. It's the same principle, though. You'll just need to make sure you calculate in direct and indirect labor costs for these added employees, and make sure you have enough work to recoup these expenses.

Not planning crew time efficiently when a company starts to grow and add employees is another major cause of business failure. Of course, a two-person lawncare team can be much more efficient than just one person for certain jobs.

Knowing when it's best to send a team out instead of just one person is critical to pricing and, ultimately, to the success of your company. When there are multiple duties that need to be done on a job site, such as mowing, hedge trimming, planting, etc. it is often advantageous to send two (or sometimes more) people to a site to reduce transportation and fuel costs. Another obvious time to send two crew members to a site is if a company applies pesticides, since the applicator has to be licensed and is often a different person than the mower/maintenance person.

What to Pay Employees

Below are average hourly wages for the first quarter of 2007 as reported by the Occupational Employment Statistics (OES) program in cooperation with the U.S. Bureau of Labor Statistics. These figures vary quite a bit from location to location, and some employees included in the statistics receive health insurance, retirement and sick leave benefits:

- Landscapers and groundskeepers: $11.53

- Tree trimmers and pruners: $14.96

A recent Canadian landscape salary survey conducted by the Canadian Immigration Service indicates that entry-level landscapers earn between $15,000 and $20,000 annually, and more experienced professionals earn between $30,000 and $45,000 annually.

Another place to check is at **www.salary.com**. You can search by job description and geographic location to find average wages in your area. Keep in mind that minimum wage laws apply across the United States and Canada. As of 2008, this is $6.55/hr (rising to $7.25/hr in 2009) in the U.S., and varies between $7.75 and $8.75 in Canada, depending on which province you're in.

5.4 Setting Your Fees

In one way, setting your fees to make money sounds pretty easy. You charge enough to recoup your actual expenses, and then beyond that, you make a decent profit. That's the general idea. But knowing how to budget such things as time and equipment wear and tear can be tricky. While in time this will all get easier, here are some tips.

5.4.1 Factors to Consider

Since rates charged and profit margins vary across the country, the best way to know how to be competitive but not undersell yourself is to find out what typical charges for services are in your area.

Call some competitors anonymously and ask what their hourly rate for general lawncare services runs. Stop by worksites you come across and ask. Talk to friends who have used other landscape services — until, of course, you came along!

As explained below, you can't just charge what others are charging. Put pen to paper and tally up the expenses specific to your company to know if you will be charging at about the average, a little lower, or a little higher.

The Dangers of Undercharging

Undercharging based on bidding too low and not calculating in a profit or overhead is a common problem for those new to the profession. It happens a lot more than overcharging does when you're just starting out.

Getting those first jobs can be almost addicting, and the thrill of the chase is on. It's easy to get caught up in the moment, not thinking about all the direct and indirect costs that are involved. You just keep hearing that final figure that someone's going to pay you over and over again in your mind, and it sounds pretty good.

Don't start too low! It's really hard to recover from that kind of mistake. Besides that, people's perception is that they get what they pay for, and lawn work is no exception. My advice is to always go for quality over being known as the low bidder in town.

Never sacrifice high standards just to get a job that you know is underpriced. Your reputation and that of your company are at stake. When you look who's still around in your profession in ten years, it's usually not the landscaper who takes shortcuts and undercut the competition.

As your reputation develops and customers clamor to you because you do such great quality work, you can inch up your profit margin.

If the project estimate comes in higher than they expected or than a client can reasonably pay, try to strike a compromise. Examples might be cutting back on the number of flats of annuals you'll be planting and caring for, or reducing the frequency you'll be providing a service such as shrub pruning, edging, and other duties that have some leeway without compromising quality.

Don't cut back on services that need to be provided on a regular schedule, such as mowing or checking an irrigation system for problems. You'll be risking problems creeping up down the line that aren't covered in the contract, as well as the integrity of your company's reputation.

Why Not Just Charge what Others Charge?

You may be tempted to just make a few calls and charge whatever the average is that your competitors charge, and not worry about plugging in figures. After all, they must have already done this. You figure you probably can't convince customers to pay you more than the average since you're the newest firm in town. But you know from reading this book that you're shortchanging yourself if you start out too low, both financially and reputation-wise.

The problem with just going with the flow like this is that your costs are going to vary, from a little to a lot. It's not a bad idea to use competitors' fees as a double-check, though, to get an idea what you can afford when you're shopping around for insurance and equipment.

If you know that you'll charge residential customers $30 an hour in your area, go through each expense you know you'll have (both fixed and variable) and keep them as low as you reasonably can. Areas where there tend to be the biggest room for shaving off dollars and still getting the same basic product are insurance and good used equipment.

Bill Baker, Founder and President of William Baker & Associates adds:

> "If covering all your costs and adding a reasonable profit margin to jobs makes you less competitive price-wise than similar companies, compete on something besides price. Customers appreciate courtesy,

professionalism, responsiveness, and assurances that the job will always be made right if they are not satisfied. Develop credibility, likeability, and trust with your customers, and they will see that your services are worth the extra cost."

5.4.2   Ways to Charge Your Fees

Knowing how you should charge your customers is very important. Choosing the right method for the right situation not only helps you judge expenses and estimate charges better, but reduces confusion to your clients who basically just want to know what the project is going to cost them. Here are some of your options, and the type of work they are best suited to.

By the Hour

If you'll be doing basic landscape maintenance work on a continual basis, it is often easiest to charge by the hour, based on a standard number of hours per month. For small residential landscapes, a client may require only three or four "person-hours" of time, while a client with a large estate might require 25 or more "person hours" each month. The client receives the same bill each month for these standard services, based on your estimate of the hours needed.

When you are estimating hourly billing, it's important to remember that there's more to the picture of routine maintenance than the actual mowing, blowing and edging time. You need to include in your hourly estimate job duties leading up to that, like:

- Loading and unloading equipment

- Rinsing tools off

- Sterilizing pruning tools

- Switching machines

- Adding gas and oil

A small residential lawn needing typical maintenance services will have a greater percentage of the time spent with all these "in-betweens."

Sample Monthly Maintenance Schedule

Here is a sample month-by-month maintenance schedule provided by Ken LaVoie, founder and owner of LaVoie Landscape Management, Inc. in Winslow, Maine. His company is a residential lawn, landscape, and snow removal business. Ken also operates Central Maine Web, a computer business that keeps him busy off season.

He says: "We keep a very tight and organized schedule to keep us focused, efficient and on task. Here's a rundown on how we do things."

April:	Spring clean up, begin edging and mulching, apply pre-emergent crabgrass preventer
May:	Begin mowing, finish edging and mulching, apply Weed n' Feed, begin planting annuals
June:	Finish planting annuals, begin "weed patrol," apply weed control or insect control, begin hedge trimming and pruning
July:	Hedge trimming, weed patrol, weeding and renovations
August:	Hedge trimming, weed patrol, insect control reapplied if needed, weed control reapplied if needed
September:	Weed n' Feed or regular fertilization, any other jobs
October:	Fall prep, remove annuals, cut perennials, apply lime, final mowing or two, plant tulip and other bulbs, catch up
November:	Fall clean up, plant tulips and other bulbs
December–March:	Wait for snow!

Flat Monthly Fee

Some lawncare specialists blend charges for occasional specialty services (see below) with normal maintenance practices, and average their costs over the season or year. Then they charge their customers the same amount of money each month. This is similar to billing hourly, except that you are prorating a whole year's worth of services.

This practice can work for or against you. It seems to work best in affluent residential areas where customers own large estates and at commercial sites rather than in typical residential neighborhoods, where some clients may not even need these services. Also, some residential customers prefer the choice of paying month by month, while in a flat monthly fee scenario, they are asked to sign a longer-term contract.

For instance, a typical residential customer will need their yard mowed and edged regularly, and probably some flowers rotated in and out of beds, and, depending on where they live, some fall clean up. Some lawns, depending on the soil, may need aeration a couple times a season to get more oxygen into the root zone and to ease compaction.

By rolling services together with regular maintenance, those with compacted soils will really stand to gain from aerification and will notice a big difference. Their lawns will be healthier and you'll probably get a referral or two.

In this case, a valuable service is provided as a given. The homeowner trusts you to take care of their needs, and doesn't mind the fact that some months are leaner than others as far as what your crew does on their property and how long they're there.

By the Job

Planting projects that are not standard monthly duties are often charged as a flat fee by the job. As an example, let's say a valued residential customer with a quarter acre backyard wants you to plant a flowerbed full of 50 flats of annuals, and asks you what you'd charge.

Figure every single cost of the equation in your head, but answer their question without getting into too many details. Give the client the final price, which includes labor, flowers (unless they're supplying them), compost or soil amendments, wear and tear and rental fees for any equipment you'll be using such as an auger and rototiller, overhead, and a reasonable profit margin.

If you spout off an hourly rate and leave your answer open-ended because you don't know how much time it will take, it can be a real turn-off. Customers prefer straightforward answers whenever possible, especially when it comes to knowing if they can afford a project or not.

That means you need to have a good idea of how much time it will take you and your crew to get all those petunias and snapdragons planted, and what all the associated costs will be so that the flat fee you quote is realistic.

Determine what tasks need to be accomplished, how long each will take, what the actual and indirect costs are, and what a reasonable profit margin is. It helps, at least initially, to write some things down. After a while, it will almost become second nature, unless you take on an entirely different kind of account than you're used to.

Also, don't hesitate to ask your wholesale nurseryperson what they estimate time-wise a planting project will take. Don't worry. In what will seem like no time, you'll be able to rattle off some pretty accurate numbers based on your own experience.

Another reason to charge by the job when doing this kind of non-routine work is so you can make sure your employees are working at a reasonable pace. If you charge by the hour for these services, your customers (and you) tend to get shorted. It's human nature. Anytime you charge by the job, you usually get the same quality job done faster, as long as you have a crew that takes pride in their work. Hire help well!

To help you when you are first starting to make these per hour estimates, use a chart that estimates how many "people hours" certain landscape jobs take. Of course, these are only averages. While these tools can be quite helpful for making ballpark estimates, keep in mind that your results will be based on the size and speed of your equipment and the skill of you workforce. There's nothing like actually timing them yourself and coming up with your own time and rate charts.

The sample People-Hour Chart on the next few pages is provided courtesy of Dr. David Hensley, Department Chair of Horticulture at University of Arkansas. The table is reprinted from *Professional Landscape Management*, Second Edition (2005, Stipes Publishing), with permission from the author.

By Area (Square Footage)

Some specialty jobs bring in a higher profit margin than routine maintenance work, just by their nature. Seasonal practices such as acrating and verticutting are examples of legitimate specialty services. The two most common ways to charge are on an area basis, or on a straight-cost basis (by the job) as explained above.

Note that it's always a good idea to charge two next-door neighbors the same price whenever possible, even if you have to slightly tip the scales to make it work. Charging one five or ten dollars more than the other based on square footage usually doesn't justify the time it took to measure the yard, and can lead to bad feelings. Neighbors really do talk over the fence — study after study has also shown that's where a typical homeowner also gets most of their lawncare advice, too. If one yard is a lot bigger, then of course you should make an adjustment.

Offering specialty services is a case where you can offer your customers a discount by getting them to help band their neighbors together so you can aerate lawns up and down the block over the course of a few days. You may even pick up new clients that hopefully will keep you around for the long haul. It's a win-win for everyone since your labor force is putting fewer miles on your trucks, you're saving money on equipment rental, and your customers are getting a better deal.

Companies that provide specialty lawncare services like aerifying usually charge between 25 and 35 cents a square foot, with a profit margin of forty percent or higher, all things considered.

Charging for Supplies

What's a fair price to charge your customers for landscape materials and supplies? About a third to half again as much as you paid (on average) from your wholesale source. This is excluding plants, which bring in more, as explained later in this section.

People-Hour Chart

Area and Operation	Average frequency per year	Average minutes per 1,000 Sq. Ft.
Turf Management		
Mowing		
21" self-propelled	30	6
36" self-propelled	30	4
48" rider	30	45 min/acre
72" rider	30	36 min/acre
Fertilization		
broadcast (PTO powered)	2	.25
36" drop spreader	2	4
Preemergent herbicide application	1	15
Postemergent herbicide application back-pack sprayer	2	15
15" boom, power	2	4
30" boom, power	2	8
Raking		
hand	1	60
power	1	10
Vacuum - 30" machine	3	10
Overseeding (machine)	1	30
Aeration (core aerator)	1	30

Edging	Linear feet	Min/1,000 linear feet
shrub bed - hand	10	60
power - walks	30	5
power - shrub beds	10	10
Trimming around objects		
string trimmer	25	10
chemical	2	10
Shrub Beds		Min./ 1,000 sq. ft.
Weeding		
hand	15	60
postemergent spot spray	3	15
Preemergent hericide application	2	5
Policing-debris removal hand	30	15
vacuum	30	7
Pruning	2	60
Fertilization (broadcast)	2	5
Mulch	1	30
Pest control - spray	2	
Trees		Min./ small tree
Pruning	2	20
Fertilization		
broadcast	2	5
deep root feed	1	30

Pest control - spray	3	15
injection	1	10
Seasonal Color Beds		**Min./ 1000 sq. ft.**
Bed preparation	1	200
Weeding (no mulch)	15	60
Cultivation (no mulch)	15	30
Mulch	1	30
Weeding (in mulch)	7	20
Pest control (spray)	3	10
Preemergent herbicide (broadcast)	1	5
Fertilization (broadcast)	2	5
Policing - debris removal - hand	25	15
vacuum	5	10
Plant removal and clean-up	1	400
Paved Areas		**Min./ 1000 sq. ft.**
Walks		
sweeping - hand	15	25
vacuum	15	4
blower	25	2
Snow removal hand	?	60
power	?	12
Drives and Parking cleaning - vacuum	10	3
snow removal	?	10

Another way to look at this is to charge no more than about ten or fifteen percent more than your customer would pay for the same items on the retail market. It pays for you to shop around to keep your costs as low as possible.

> TIP: You can also save money on supplies if you generate your own compost from lawn and yard trimmings, and buy material in bulk whenever possible.

When opportunities to plant something for your customers come up, try to supply the actual plants whenever you can. Suggest this before your customers go to the local nursery and get their own. There is usually between a 75 and 100% profit margin supplying plants. Note that this doesn't mean that a flat of pansies your customer would have to pay $15 for would cost them $30; buying plants from a wholesale nursery gives you a sizable price break.

Another good reason you should offer to supply the plants is that it keeps you in control of the project. You can make sure that high-quality plants are chosen, and planted in a timely way. As mentioned in Chapter 2, customers tend to pick flats that are fullest in bloom without thinking about checking the root system, and might have their own ideas about when to get them planted.

5.4.3   Getting Paid

Invoices

Invoices are basically bills sent to your customers after contractual work has been completed, or is in process. There are different types of invoices used in the landscape industry. The simplest invoices are mailed out each month and the same amount of money is due each time, based on agreed-upon routine maintenance services, such as mowing, edging and shaping and trimming of shrubs. An example of this kind of invoice appears on the next page.

Other invoices include planting and specialty services such as aerifying, verticutting, flowerbed rotation, or fall clean up, which may be charged on a square-foot basis or by the job. They are not billed routinely each month, and may arrive at any time based on agreed-upon services and schedules. They are sent after work is completed. On the next page is an example of this kind of invoice, in which service for scheduled monthly maintenance is also included.

Sample Basic Service Invoice

(On Your Letterhead)

Invoice #: 100-000-021

Date: June 30, 2009
Date Due: July 30, 2009

Customer: Jane Jones
123 Main Street
Sunnyday, CA 90211

SERVICE PERFORMED	DATE	PRICE
Routine Maintenance *(Mowing, Edging, Trimming)*	6/1/2009 - 6/30/2009	$140.00
TOTAL – PLEASE PAY THIS AMOUNT		$140.00

Payment due in 30 days. Thank you for your prompt payment!

Whatever style of invoice you use, they should reflect language of the contract that was signed between you and your client. This isn't the time to decide to increase your profit by 20% and see if anyone notices.

True, cost of materials, labor, supplies and everything else goes up over time, but these increases shouldn't just magically show up on a bill. They should be discussed ahead of time, in person if possible, with each client. If you and a customer signed a contract stipulating that you'd perform certain services at a set rate over a 12-month period, you need to honor your commitment, unless a potential change was spelled out. Wait to raise prices until the next time around.

Large projects that extend over several months are often billed based on milestones when certain goals are reached. Most state laws stipulate that you can charge up to but not exceeding a set amount (10 percent is common) of the cost of a project before work commences. A final lump sum payment is due at the completion of the work.

Often, large projects have minor changes from the original contract that need to be made due to lack of availability of a specified type or brand of material, plant or anything else. In this case, you need to have what's called a "change order" document that details the changes, and is signed by both parties.

TIP: You should also make sure that you spell out in the contract when remittance of any bill is considered delinquent. You can legally stop work if you're not getting paid in a timely way.

Sample Detailed Service Invoice

(On Your Letterhead)

Invoice #: 100-000-022

Date: June 30, 2009
Date Due: July 30, 2009

Customer: Jane Jones
123 Main Street
Sunnyday, CA 90211

SERVICE PERFORMED	DATE	PRICE
Planted Flowerbed *(provided 10 flats @ $15 each)*	6/4/2009	$250.00
Aerated Lawn	6/8/2009	$100.00
Fertilized Lawn *(provided 40 pounds of ammonium sulfate @ $35)*	6/15/2009	$100.00
Monthly Maintenance	6/1/2009 - 6/30/2009	$200.00
TOTAL – PLEASE PAY THIS AMOUNT		$650.00

Payment due in 30 days. Thank you for your prompt payment!

Be forewarned. If you contract with the government, you may have to wait a while to get paid. But, you eventually will! Also, if you ever go into subcontracting work, you'll often have to wait 30 days to get the last invoice paid due to lien laws. Make sure to send receipts to your customers promptly when invoices are paid.

Methods of Payment

Landscapers these days accept many forms of payment, including checks, cash, and credit cards. Some are even getting very modern and accepting payments using PayPal (**www.paypal.com**), an electronic form of payment that accepts checks, credit cards or cash and makes an electronic deposit into the designated account.

Any time credit card charges are accepted, expect to pay a small service charge, based on a percentage of the sale. Check with your bank or one of the many private companies out there about getting a merchant account set up. Shop around for the best surcharge rate possible, but expect to be charged at least 2 percent. Many landscapers reluctantly accept credit card payments because they're worried they'll lose the client otherwise.

Avoiding Delinquent Accounts

Avoidance is a big key here. Try to politely remind your customers who are delinquent paying a bill as gently as possible that their payment is due. Use the word "due" the first time rather than "late," since this gives them a face-saving way out.

This can be done in person when you or one of your employees is on the job site (don't have more than one person confront them, though) or over the phone. Another face-saving tactic that often gets you paid is to ask them if they received the invoice. Do this even if you're pretty sure they have and just haven't gotten around to paying. Ask if they'd like another copy. Make sure that you just happen to have one with you if you're on the job site.

Give them a week to pay you, and call one more time. If they don't answer the phone but have an answering machine, leave a polite but very clear message that you'd like them to call you about service they received. Although you're probably tempted, avoid leaving a message for the whole group to hear at their cocktail party that night about how rude and selfish they are for not paying you and avoiding your calls.

If you still don't get a response, you can do one of two things. You can stop work on the site until they pay their debt, or you can provide them "courtesy service" for a while longer. In either case, it's time to get a little more formal.

Send a certified letter along with another copy of the invoice. Wait another week. Hopefully, this will take care of the problem. Perhaps they've been out of town or had something more important (at least to them) on their mind, like a family illness, divorce, or any number of things that can distract people.

If they've been a good, solid customer and this is out of character for them, be particularly cautious about jumping to any conclusions. No, it's not right that you haven't been paid, but the goal is to get paid, not win a power struggle.

If all those measures have failed, you need to definitely stop work on the site if you haven't already, and decide whether it's a big enough bill to warrant taking legal action. It can cost more money than it's sometimes worth to chase after a $40 payment.

If a customer owes in the hundreds of dollars, it's an easier choice. Take action with a series of "notice letters" when the 30-day point comes and goes. You can send them incrementally over the course of a few weeks. Forms are available online or from your attorney. Obviously, check with your lawyer as well, if it gets to the point where you really are serious about taking legal action.

5.5   Being Professional on the Job

Professionalism is extremely important in this business. Your personal involvement developing excellent client relationships is vital, in addition to everyday efforts by any field crew you might have. It may seem like a lot of work developing client relationships and calling people who don't have a problem with your service, but you'll soon discover that going the extra mile is key to retaining clients. Look at it this way:

it's a lot less work keeping the clients you have happy than having to beat the pavement to find new ones.

Also, Bill Baker, Founder and President of William Baker & Associates, suggests that you be professional off the job as well:

> "Assume you are always being watched and evaluated by others. After all, customers are also likely to be found through your social circles, your children's sporting events, where you shop, and through groups with whom you share a common interest."

5.5.1   Developing Client Trust

Take every opportunity you can to earn the trust of each and every one of your customers, from the one with the smallest account to the one with the largest. Trust develops over time and isn't something that just happens on its own. You know that your company will be honorable and trustworthy in all dealings with clients, but you've got to prove it to them.

Here are some tried and true guidelines for developing a long-term trusting relationship with your customers.

1. Show up on time.

Even if you know you'll stay a little late to get the job at hand done, if you arrive late to a worksite, it gives the impression that you're untrustworthy and trying to cheat the customer out of hours.

Some clients really will complain if your crew arrives five minutes late, especially during what they view as the "trial period." The best way around this is to schedule maintenance work and projects over a certain period of time (e.g., "We'll be out every Tuesday morning,") rather than assign an exact start time when at all possible.

For instance, if you've got a crew going out to perform routine lawncare duties at Mrs. Black's estate that you charge her two hours of time a week for, make sure the contract stipulates that the work will be performed "over a two-hour period" each Monday morning rather than specifying the exact time. She probably won't even notice the exact time the crew is there if the contract's written up that way. Of course, exercise common courtesy and ask your clients if certain time periods are better for them than others.

There are instances when you have to be on time or your reputation will be on the line. These are for appointments with potential customers, and follow-up meetings with clients. Be punctual. It shows respect for your client and underlines the professionalism of your company.

2. Always do what you say you will.

This covers things such as being on time to meetings, using the quality and quantity of products you specified in the contract without skimping, following recommended horticulture practices and procedures, and visiting job sites often enough to avoid potential problems.

The landscape industry, as you know, is a service industry, and much of what you spend your time doing is keeping landscapes as attractive and healthy as possible. Sometimes it can be pretty tempting to cut a corner to get the job done a little early and head out to that ball game you've been looking forward to. Plan ahead so you can do both!

Don't wait until the last minute to start what you know will be a big project. I know this sounds obvious, but it's a very common occurrence. A two-person mowing, edging and weeding project that you've charged your customer a half-day for should take about a half of a day.

Planning your time based on how long a project will actually take improves and gets easier with practice. Until you have more experience of your own, use the labor "people-hour" chart I provided earlier as a sample to "ballpark" how long projects will take.

You'll learn soon enough how much actual time you should schedule your crew for after repeating the same job in several different situations. In the meantime, include a fudge factor of about 10% more time than you think you'll need to make sure you can get the job done in the designated time period.

If Friday rolls around and you've got 10 estate-size lawns all over town to do, and two people to get everything finished, there's been a mistake made somewhere. The worst part of it is that customers will notice something like their lawn not getting mowed when it should have been, and some won't cut you a lot of slack.

It's kind of ironic, but you need customers to give you a little leeway when you're starting out, because you're new at all this. But, in their eyes, they may just see things the other way. Since you're new, they think they'd better keep their eye on you!

When circumstances prevent you form performing a task that you promised in a timely way, get a hold of your clients right away to explain the situation and give them an update of when you can get it done. Not hearing anything is what scares them.

3. Provide reliable follow-through.

Providing follow-through means keeping track of all projects past and present, and making sure clients are satisfied with the service they have received. If they are not satisfied, you need to look for measurable yet economical ways to make things right with them.

If you are good at what you do, before you know it you will have acquired lots of customers. If you have a crew, they're undoubtedly doing excellent work and are getting more experienced every day. You're starting to get lots of referrals. You're making enough money to buy some upgraded equipment. Things are going well! You're really making a go of your company. Sometimes about now it's easy to start getting spread a little thin and losing track of what needs to be done.

Make sure you keep a log of what projects are scheduled for each client, and when your crew is expected next at each job site. Keep a copy in your vehicles so every employee has access to it.

Now is not the time to back off on service! It's great to grow your company, but don't lose sight of the importance of keeping your current customers happy. Personally call or drop by once in a while, even when things seem to be on track.

Another aspect of providing good follow-through relates to staying ahead of potential horticulture problems, like disease and insect outbreaks. Remember that preventing these pests by taking good care of the plants through proper watering, fertilizing and doing whatever other duties need to be done on a regular basis is one of the most important services you can offer.

While you may not feel appreciated at the time since things look good and you're not hearing any customer feedback, know that you might just be preventing a disaster. Just talk to someone who's experienced the opposite. Letting a problem get out of hand and ending up with brown spots all over the lawn that you don't even know about until an upset customer calls you can take away months of respect and trust.

Develop solid relationships with professionals in closely related fields that you don't have expertise in, and don't hesitate to call on them if and when problems develop. Know at least one respected Certified or Consulting Arborist, Certified Irrigation Auditor, and Pest Control Advisor that you can call on. Don't hesitate to pay them a consulting fee (this should always be built into your costs of doing business that you pass on to your customers) when problems develop.

Minimally, have your own crew trained to look for the beginning signs and symptoms of problems, and have them suggest to the customer that they call a specialist right away. I advise you to think about contracting these professionals out yourself as you grow your company. It gives you even more assurance of taking care of problems early on, which can get tougher as you hire more employees and have them scattered to several job sites.

I can't overemphasize the importance of making sure your customers are fully satisfied with the service they're getting. Many successful landscape company owners with crews that generally service the clients make a practice of personally calling each customer once every month or two just to make sure they are happy with how things are going.

Others mail personal thank-you cards with satisfaction surveys inside and a stamped envelope to conveniently return them in. Do whatever makes sense to you to let your particular client base know that you value their business and will continue to offer excellent service.

Be sure to actually read and pay attention to any surveys that are returned! If several customers bring up the same issue, assume it's a real concern you need to deal with quickly. Even if just one customer has a suggestion, take it seriously, at least as it relates to their situation.

A Success Story:
Donna Burdick, D&J Landscape Contractors

Donna Burdick is the owner and founder of D&J Landscape Contractors in Portland, Oregon, a landscape contracting/maintenance business serving the Portland/Vancouver area. She runs the business with another female co-owner, Jamie Hansen.

What is a typical workday like for Donna? Starting at 6 a.m. she answers emails and phone calls, and makes sure that materials will be delivered on time, while simultaneously lining up work crews and assigning daily tasks. From mid-morning to mid-afternoon, she performs sales and management tasks. Then, through the evening, Donna has appointments with clients, checks on projects, and visits job sites. Her business partner Jamie is the field supervisor, and is onsite 85% of the time.

A love of plants and the outdoors, along with a strong desire for self-employment, convinced Donna to shift gears after following an entirely different route. She graduated from the University of Oregon in 1986 with a degree in Sociology and a certificate in Women's Studies, and worked as a case manager at a family shelter. With somewhat flexible hours, she was able to start a landscape maintenance business on the side, following her desire and passion to pursue a career in horticulture.

After working in landscape maintenance for awhile, Donna made a decision to concentrate on landscape contracting to allow for "more creativity and to work on bigger projects." D&J Landscape Contractors currently brings in about 80% of its gross earnings from the contract end of the business and employs four full-time and two or three part-time workers during the season. Off-season, Donna "reassesses the year" and takes time to "touch base with clients." D&J Landscape Contractors also sets up display gardens at home and garden shows in Portland to drum up seasonal business.

What does it take to make it as one of the five percent female landscape contractors in the state of Oregon? "Hard work, and building and developing trust and one-on-one relationships with clients," says Donna.

She says her background in the social sciences has served her landscape career well. Her particular skills are "in the ability to organize the numerous details that go into manifesting a perfectly suited landscape, including effectively managing crew, sub-contractors, landscape designers, and architects. I provide my clients with assurance that everything's taken care of, and they'll receive an end result they're proud of."

What sets D&J Landscape Contractors apart from the competition? Making the experience of home improvement one that people value and by paying attention to details. "We encourage our client's ideas and dreams from beginning to end, and communicate with them throughout the process."

At the end of the day, what satisfies Donna about her work is "the heartfelt satisfaction my clients receive by having a beautifully landscaped home. Although the amount of joy plants and flowers provide isn't necessarily a surprise to me, it is to them once they see the immense difference small updates can make. To me, witnessing reinvigorated pride in a home is an accomplishment."

It's no surprise that D&J Landscape Contractors is a community-oriented company that has donated time and materials planting gardens of all kinds, including working on Habitat for Humanity projects.

5.5.2 Communicating with Clients

Communicating clearly and effectively with your clients starts with the very first time you contact them — whether it's through the mail, door-to-door canvassing, or a phone call. If you do it well, you'll attract and keep customers much more easily than if it's a hit-and-miss activity you do from time to time without much planning. Stay in close communication with your customers and listen to what they have to say.

Ken LaVoie, founder and owner of LaVoie Landscape Management, Inc. in Winslow, Maine, has an excellent way of keeping his clients informed of what he's doing. He keeps his schedule posted on his website. He values his customers and knows the importance of communication.

Bill Baker, Founder and President of William Baker and Associates, has this to offer: "A lack of communication can lead the customer to negative speculation. Failure to explain what is happening can leave people thinking the worst. If it is a commercial client, you can create an awkward situation for the contracts manager or your contact person in the customer's organization."

Things can take a downward spiral quickly when communication starts falling through the cracks. The situation can easily slip up on you before you even realize what is going on.

Let's say your crew has shown up at a valued customer's house on their assigned day and done a great job with the contracted tasks, but you still get a complaint from the customer out of the blue. Well, at least to you it seems like it's out of the blue. What possibly could have gone wrong?

Any number of things, but don't rule out what your client might view as a lack of necessary communication being the root of the problem. With more and more dual-career couples at work and retirees living longer and traveling more, fewer people are home when contracted work is being done.

You know your crew has been there. They certainly can vouch for this, but a client may still question if they're getting a good value for their money if they never hear from you or the company representative who spent so much time with them initially to get them to sign the contract in the first place.

There are a couple of take-home messages here. First, doing the best job possible helps defuse a difficult situation quite a bit. When Mr. and Mrs. Gomez get home from their vacation and notice how nice their lawn and flowerbeds look, that's like giving you a pat on the back. They see the results of your hard work.

However, over time they might start to take their beautiful yard for granted, as a given, and wonder why, with all that money they're sending you every month, you don't at least give them a courtesy call now and them. You may never get an actual complaint, but your trust is on the line.

This fact may not seem fair. Maybe it isn't. But many people want some pretty constant reassurance that you're personally still around. This can create a bit of a quagmire. You can't (and shouldn't) be expected to personally kiss babies and shake hands all day long, but you'd be surprised at how welcome a phone message left on a busy couple's answering machine or a quick stop off at the home of a valued elderly client once in a while can be.

Stopping by once in awhile can be a quick yet effective way of letting your clients know that you're serious about providing the quality of service you promised, and want to make sure things are going well. You should be particularly attentive to follow-up if your crew is not fluent in the dominant language of your clients. Many landscape company owners have found that spending as few as two hours a week making these kinds of calls can save double or triple that many hours chasing down complaints that otherwise would occur.

Also remember that one bad apple can spoil the whole crate. Research has shown that on average, a disgruntled customer badmouths your company to six other people. Some customers find it hard (or embarrassing) to be direct and ask you about what they perceive as negligence on your end, but will unleash to a friend. Don't let word-of-mouth work against you! It can and should be your closest ally.

A Success Story: Heaviland Enterprises, Inc.

Heaviland Enterprises, Inc., founded by Ron and Tom Heaviland in 1985, uses a combination of active communication skills that include such routine practices as performance surveys, active listening, an emergency service number, and follow-up calls to service requests. Today, the company employs more than 100 people, and maintains 170 commercial sites.

Tom humbly says he "fell into this business." He and his dad purchased a small commercial maintenance company in the San Diego, California, area 20 years ago. Tom earned a Bachelor's degree in Business Administration, and says his horticulture skills were limited to shoveling snow.

Tom picked up speed quickly, though, in California by becoming a Certified Landscape Technician (CLT) through the California Landscape Contractor's Association, a Certified Irrigation Auditor through the Irrigation Association, and a Certified Landscape Professional (CLP) through the Associated Landscape Contractors of America (now PLANET).

Tom's philosophy has paid off, both in profits and recognition. Heaviland Enterprises, Inc. has won numerous awards for their high-quality work, earning the Torch Award for Ethics in the Workplace from the Better Business Bureau in 2002 (finalist in 2001); being nationally recognized in 2004 as one of "20 Great Organizations" in the green industry by Landscape Management magazine; and being featured in the Professional Landscape Network (PLANET) "Successcapes," a monthly article featuring successful landscape companies worldwide.

6. Getting Clients

Using good marketing skills is crucial to getting business. Marketing is the way that you present your landscaping services to potential clients. You can use a variety of free and paying methods to get your name out there, and it's a good idea to try a variety of methods to see what works best for you.

When you are designing your marketing materials, think about what consumers look for when choosing a professional landscaper. By far the top criterion is "good references and reputation," as reported by 67% of a recent Gallup Poll's participants.

Does this mean that only companies that have been around for decades will likely be hired? No, in fact the length of time a company has been in business was ranked as a priority by only 32.9% of respondents of the same survey. Think of your first customer as your first good reference, and over time, you'll have many clients who will vouch for your professionalism.

Bill Baker, Founder and President of William Baker & Associates says:

> "Make a good impression before people even meet you. Hire a graphic artist and work with a good commercial printing service to develop first-rate brochures, stationery, and business cards. These materials often precede a direct introduction to you and your company. Further, develop an appealing, informative, user-friendly website that explains your services to potential customers."

Here are some ideas on how to sell your services to potential clients.

6.1   Types of Clients

Many very successful landscape company owners choose to work in the residential maintenance market segment, finding that they enjoy the diversity of working at several sites, like its personal nature, and have more work than they can handle in a few years.

Some landscape company owners have told me that they can't imagine being happy working on large commercial maintenance ventures, while others who have followed this route are quite satisfied. The key is to follow your passion. If you've followed the suggestions so far, you'll have the expertise in horticulture and business to succeed at whichever path you decide to take.

6.1.1   Residential Clients

If your landscape company is going to specialize in yard and lawn maintenance, you can offer services such as mowing, aerating, edging, power sweeping, raking, fertilizing, mulching and rotating flowers, verticutting, and light shrub and small tree pruning.

If you decide to get a landscape contractor's license, you'll have much more freedom to do whatever it is your residential clients ask you to do without turning away business. By definition, a landscape contractor installs plants and may install water features, irrigation systems, fences, decks, driveways, walkways, retaining walls and lighting for compensation. An added incentive to become a licensed contractor is that some states require this if you provide services, plants, and labor totaling $500 or more per job.

Usually, the company owner or a lead employee, but not both, are required to be licensed with the state contractors' board if any building or substantial non-maintenance work will be done. Most states require between two and four years of experience (often, education counts toward a portion or all this requirement) before you're eligible to take the contractor exam. Also, if you'll be applying pesticides, you'll need a state license as well.

It can be a great feeling to get your contractor's license and not have to tell a potential customer that you're sorry you can't install that irrigation system they ask you to since you can't legally do it as a gardener.

6.1.2   Commercial Clients

Commercial landscape maintenance offers great potential for some landscape company owners. Clients include retail shopping centers, strip malls and malls, office parks, banks and other financial institutions, resort hotels, homeowner associations, gated retirement communities, managed care facilities, private hospitals, private schools, churches and synagogues, private golf courses, auto centers/malls, restaurants and fast food establishments, theme parks, and even movie and television sets.

In some cases, commercial clients will want you to provide general landscaping services that include just about everything you're trained, licensed, and certified to do, and in others your client may contract you to perform a single service. Based on your expertise, this could be lawncare, arboriculture, or installing and maintaining water or lighting features.

The profit you'll make in the commercial sector varies widely, as it does for residential work. It depends on the size of the contracted site and your specific duties and scope of work. A very large account might net you a few thousand dollars monthly, while smaller ones may bring in a couple hundred dollars.

While you can increase your earnings this way, getting a commercial account usually involves bidding on projects, which is as much an art as a science and takes years of experience to get really good at.

As far as the actual work involved, commercial accounts are often easier to maintain because the physical area you and your crew are working in is larger. They're easier to mow, edge, and fertilize and to get equipment in and out of. And, you can keep crew expenses down since they're on the road fewer hours and their activities are often more coordinated and efficient. Vehicular insurance rates go down, too, since there are fewer miles driven over the course of a year. But, because everything's on a larger scale, mistakes can be, too. If you misjudge expenses or the actual time a job will take and you're stuck with honoring a too-low bid, the result can spell disaster.

If you do decide to venture into the commercial sector, start cautiously. Don't jump into it all at once. If your resources are all tied up in a couple commercial accounts and you've either underbid or something holds up a payment owed you, you're stuck.

Here are some things to consider before you take the plunge:

- Do you have enough experience bidding to be assured that if you get the job, you haven't sold yourself short?

- Do you have the right equipment (industrial with enough horse-power) and enough of it to get the job done professionally and on time? Do you have the means to lease what you don't have and will need?

- Do you have adequate personnel to do the job in a timely way? Will other loyal customers be sacrificed and will you risk losing their business if you reallocate your crew?

While buying supplies in bulk can save you money, it's easy to over or underestimate the amount you'll need at any site, and on a larger one, your mistakes are amplified. If you bid too low, you may also find yourself having to cut corners to keep your head above water, which can leave the site looking less than your professional best and turn off potential new customers driving by as well as the contact who hired you.

6.2 Marketing to Residential Clients

Especially when you are first starting out, residential clients will likely make up the bulk of your business. Here are some ideas on how to spread awareness of your services, and help people make the decision to hire you.

6.2.1   Referrals and Word-of-Mouth

Recent findings by the Associated Landscape Contractors of America (ALCA, now PLANET) indicate that referrals from family members or friends are the number-one method of choice (55%) used by people hiring landscape professionals.

Referrals are the most cost-effective promotion there is, too. They're absolutely free! How do you get referrals? Do such a great job with your current customers that they can't help gloating about your services. When you meet with clients, smile and say something simple but sincere, using your customer's name whenever possible, like, "Good morning, Mrs. Smith!" Use the more formal last name unless you've been told to call them by their first name. Don't talk too long, though. After all, you've got a job to do.

Keeping employee spirits high and promoting a spirit of teamwork and cooperation will also help. In many cases, it's more likely that your clients will be talking more to your crew than to you. Make sure you train crewmembers who will have contact with your customers how to address them and treat them with respect.

You can also hand out pens, rulers, notepads, etc. with your company name and contact information on them. My favorite technique is to hand out high-quality magnets — not the too-cheap kind that fall right off the refrigerator. Family, friends and neighbors will tend to see this more often than any other freebie.

> **TIP:**   Some businesses will offer clients a discount on their own services if they refer a friend.

Here are some more important standards you should set for your company right off the bat. They are crucial for keeping customers happy and maximizing referrals. You can also review section 5.5 on professionalism on the job for more ideas:

- Always treat your customers with respect.

- Listen intently. Make eye contact and stand facing them without your arms crossed when you're conversing.

- Be honest. If your customer requests a service that you know they don't need, offer a better alternative. Even if you lose money, you may more than make up for it by increasing their confidence and trust in you.

- Make sure a professional answers your company's phone during stated business hours. If you need to, forward calls to your cell phone rather than not having a person available to do this.

- Return phone calls and emails promptly.

- Make sure your phone message machine is on during off hours. Clearly state your company name and the fact that you're sorry you missed their call, and a request that they leave their full name and phone number and time of day you should return their call.

- Provide services on time and in a professional way. Always stay ahead of potential problems such as diseases, insects, dangerous limbs, etc.

- Think like a Boy Scout: Always leave your "campsite" cleaner when you leave than when you arrived! Do a little extra from time to time, like picking up a piece of trash that blew into a customer's yard, rolling in their emptied trash cans, or putting their newspaper by their front door.

6.2.2   Advertising

In the same ALCA study mentioned earlier, advertising and the phone book were tied as the second-most common way (22%) potential customers find you. I've talked to lots of landscape company owners about effective and not-so-effective advertising.

Almost unanimously, high points are given to distributing neighborhood flyers and using mailers in a localized area not too far from your company's headquarters, especially in large metropolitan areas. It's easy to understand why. You put fewer miles on your vehicles, and you and your crew spend less time on the road. Customers get these savings passed on to them since your overhead is lower.

Also, if there's a problem such as disease or insect outbreak in the neighborhood, you will probably notice it faster since it's in your territory. If there's an emergency like a faithful customer reporting a broken sprinkler resembling Old Faithful, you can take care of it sooner.

What kinds of mailers work? Many successful landscapers use small ones that are printed and packaged along with a dozen or so others and mailed to targeted neighborhoods by specialty houses. This can be very cost-effective and can really work. These mailers are mostly full of nail salon, carpet cleaning, and oil/lube job ads, so you shouldn't have too much competition.

Also, developing a personalized brochure or flyer for your business can be a great way to attract new customers and to keep current customers aware of other services you offer that they may not have previously considered. You can distribute flyers yourself door-to-door in an afternoon or two, or hire someone to deliver them.

Your flyer should include your company's name, logo, all contact information (including website if you have one) and a list of services offered. The key with flyers (and all advertising, really) is to include enough information to entice the reader without turning them off with too much text.

For services most people are familiar with, such as mowing and planting bedding plants, no further explanation is needed. But rather than just list the fact that you "aerate lawns," it's much better to state a benefit, like that you "improve drainage and reduce thatch by aerating lawns." Whenever you add or expand services, be sure to update your flyer and website too.

TIP: Including helpful free landscape advice in your advertising makes it something the customer is more likely to hold onto. Think about including a monthly list of gardening tips, for example.

Here are a couple of bad ideas that can aggravate people more than attract their business: putting flyers under car windshields, and dropping a business card on the ground next to somebody's front door. I know people who will purposely avoid hiring anyone doing this.

Yellow Pages

What about the local phone directory? This can be a very powerful tool. Minimally, consider placing a standard size listing under the most specific heading you can based on your services. For instance, if you're just doing lawncare, place your ad under the lawncare section if there is one. There are almost always landscaping and gardening headings, too.

There are conflicting reports on the success of running large Yellow Pages ads. No doubt, these are expensive. Do they catch the eye of potential customers? Maybe. Some companies swear by it, while others just as adamantly advise against it, and have pulled ads themselves after getting no more business from them than they did without them.

My suggestion is to do your own feasibility study. Take about ten minutes to look through the ads yours would be competing against in your local phone book. Are there lots of large paid ads? A few? None?

You can also call four or five non-landscape businesses that took out medium and large ads. Consider calling non-competitive but related companies that could help drum up business for you. Examples are general contractors that do home remodeling work, plumbers, and pool services. These people come face to face with many potential landscape customers.

Ask them directly if they think the ad has brought them much business. They generally are flattered you asked and not standoffish — after all, you're not a competitor trying to steal some of their turf. When wrapping up the call, ask them to keep your contact info handy, or offer to send them some business cards.

After talking to other business owners, you should be in a good position to decide which direction to take. If you're still unsure, go the conservative route and start off your first year with the smallest ad possible under the most likely category your prospective customers would look under.

Signage

Finally, don't underestimate the importance of putting your company name and contact information (phone number and website) on the side of your trucks. For a few hundred dollars, you can bring in lots of customers by doing this.

Just think how many people otherwise would pass by your work sites each day, impressed with your work but having no idea who did it or how to contact you. It's also a good idea to have a few words that describe the services you offer on the signage.

6.2.3   Get Some Publicity

The ideas below will help get your name out there and some are even free. Don't be afraid to spend (as long as you budget for it) a little bit of money on the right promotion. You'll get a tax write-off for it, too.

Volunteer for a Good Cause

It will not only warm your heart and help your local community, but will allow you to meet like-minded citizens, many of whom have homes of their own that could use a little landscaping. You might even get your company's name listed in the local newspaper and your picture in the "society page," and in the sponsoring charity's newsletter.

Adopt a Highway

Contact your local state department of highways and offer to sponsor trash clean-up along a portion of a well-traveled thoroughfare, preferably in an area you want to drum up business. In most cases, you'll get a free sign installed in the section you'll be responsible for, recognizing your company as the good Samaritan.

Of course, you'll need to agree to keep the area assigned clean, or if you prefer, you can hire out the actual work for a couple hundred dollars a month. But, whether you and your employees do the upkeep or you farm it out, make sure you hold up your end of the bargain. An unkempt highway stretch full of cups and beer cans under your company's name is as harmful as bad word-of-mouth.

Sponsor a Youth League Sports Team

If you have a child playing amateur sports, this could be a natural. You won't miss a game and your company logo and company name will be prominently displayed on banners and uniforms, and in written and online team information. This is also a perfect opportunity for you to offer suggestions to the city parks department for improving the field if you notice problems. Be careful not to badmouth the current company's work — it might be owned by the parent of another child on the team. In many cases, cities contract out field maintenance. They may even be soliciting bids soon!

Industry or Business-Related Involvement

Another great way of promoting your business is to get involved in green industry associations. Many of them have both hard copy and online directories they make available to residential and commercial potential customers. Join one or two that especially interest you and blend in well with your goals and skills. Many association member-ships include complimentary trade journal subscriptions and other benefits. Refer to section 3.2 for a list of several choices.

There are dozens of other opportunities out there to get you noticed while being a good citizen and making a difference. Think about:

- Sponsoring (or co-sponsoring with related businesses) residential Christmas tree recycling or fall clean up days at a local park

- Serving on your local parks commission

- Sponsoring a tree-planting ceremony on Arbor Day

- Participating in a service club, such as Rotary or Lion's

6.2.4   Your Website

How important is getting a company website? I think it's very impor-tant in this day and age. If a potential client has heard good things about you, or drove by one of your worksites and noticed your truck with your company name on it, he or she will often just try to find you online. If you're nowhere to be found in cyberspace, you may be losing customers you don't even know about.

The mere fact that you have a web presence shows you're progressive and leads people to believe that you're on the cutting edge of your pro-fession. In other words, it is a great image-builder. Additionally, potential customers can find you when they search green industry sites looking for local landscapers. Many, many people hire landscape companies this way these days.

There are almost limitless possibilities how you can use four or five pages of online space to promote your company and your services. Customers and potential customers will be impressed with all that knowledge you have on your site.

A Great Example to Follow

Borst Landscape and Design was the brainchild of President and Founder Mark C. Borst, who opened up shop in Wyskoff, New Jersey in 1989. The first few years, Mark operated his company part time while pursuing a degree in Landscape Architecture and Ornamental Horticulture. Since 1993, Mark has operated his company on a full-time basis, and added the organic lawn care program in 1995. In 2002, Borst Landscape and Design moved to its current headquarters in Allentown, New Jersey.

Due to its success and professionalism, Borst was ranked one of *Landscape Magazine*'s 20 Great Companies in 2004. And, for very good reasons! This rapidly growing company now employs 60 professionals, and earned revenues exceeding 4 million dollars in 2004. Borst Landscape and Design has also earned repeated awards in the "Residential and Commercial Landscape Maintenance" category from the New Jersey Landscape Contractors' Association.

Borst Landscape and Design maintains an excellent, user-friendly website (**www.borstlandscape.com**) that includes a quarterly newsletter complete with president's message welcoming reader feedback, seasonal tips, Borst's work calendar, and click-on photos of a wide array of plants they include in their designs. Take a look to open your mind to great possibilities!

Mark Borst's dream to own a successful, reputable landscape company has been realized, thanks to his vision, perseverance and excellent customer service.

Getting your Website Built

You can either hire a professional to design and set a website up for you (expect to pay a few thousand dollars), or build one yourself using any one of several web design software products out there such as Microsoft FrontPage, or Register.com's WebSiteNOW.

Personally, I recommend that you start out building your own, at least to begin with. You might be surprised how professional you can make your site look. And, it will get you online in a hurry — often within an hour or two from the time you begin the design process depending on how extensive you want your initial website to be. If, on down the line, you want a more high-tech site, you can always hire a web designer.

To go the do-it-yourself route, which includes registering your domain name, the actual website and email service costs approximately $120 to $150 a year. If you sign up for multiple years, the price goes down considerably. Those are some pretty reasonable rates for promoting your company and advertising your services.

You can register your company name as your website domain name, and link the first names of your key employees to it for receiving and sending email.

6.3   Marketing to Commercial Clients

Getting one or two commercial jobs to complement your residential business can boost your company's profits on your terms. You may find that you really enjoy the nature of the work. If you work hard and do high-quality work that gets noticed, you may decide this is the best niche for your company and grow in this direction. On the other hand, if it's not your cup of tea, you won't lose your shirt if you start out with moderation.

Before you spend time driving all over the place to lots of commercial sites to look for clients, slow down and make sure you're really ready to play in the big leagues. Probably the biggest risk you'll face is relying too much on one or two large contracts. It's kind of like planting a single species of landscape tree, only to have it wiped out by something as devastating as Dutch elm disease.

I suggest that you start off very conservatively and see how one or two multi-acreage projects of moderate scope go, in as close to your area of expertise as possible. Maintain the residential end as your "bread and butter" until you're sure you're prepared to handle larger contracts.

How do you find potential commercial customers? Here are your best bets:

- Referrals from friends and business associates

- Postings on green industry association job boards

- Classified advertisements

- Your own highly tailored flyers and mailers

- Phone calls and drop in visits to potential clients

I suggest that if you want to break into the commercial market, you start off by openly telling your retail clients that you're interested in expanding in this way. Make sure they know you're not going to pull the rug out from under them, though! Ask for their help and referrals. Many landscape company owners have to actually turn down commercial contracts after a while because this becomes almost too effective. Here are some other strategies for landing commercial contracts.

6.3.1 Meeting with Decision Makers

It's rare to get a commercial job without having to compete against other bidders. It's just the nature of the work. It helps to win the bid if you get to know potential clients personally in advance. They'll remember you if you've stopped by and made a good impression before bids come in — especially if you took it upon yourself to contact them.

Often, commercial sites are contracted over a two or three year period. Finding out when a bid is coming up and calling the person in charge a few months before it will be officially "advertised" is a good tactic. Being assertive can really set you apart from the rest.

Make a list of potential customers. This can be anything from noting poorly maintained sites you see driving around town, to getting names of establishments from the Internet or the phone book. Any place there are plants that need to be maintained there's a potential job. Do some checking and find out who the person is with the power to hire your company and call them personally, requesting a short meeting on the premises.

How to Prepare

Make sure you schedule the meeting soon, but after you have time to drive out on your own and walk the property and make notes of what services you can offer based on the specific needs of the site and your expertise.

Type out some notes on your letterhead so you can hand your suggestions to your potential client at the meeting. Make sure you address this person by their name in all correspondence, rather than "to whom it may concern." At this point, it's best not to attach a price to the hardcopy, but you'd better have a good idea how much you'll need to charge to cover your costs.

When you head out, bring your resume, business cards and pictures you have that feature your best work. If you've done other commercial work, concentrate on talking that up over your residential experience.

Some landscapers swear by the use of a portfolio of photos showcasing their work at various sites to get additional work. As you grow your company, you might want to invest in one as well. Digital cameras are becoming more and more affordable and chronicling your projects with before-and-after shots is always a good idea — and great for your website.

At the Meeting

Let's say you're able to schedule a meeting with Mary Smith at a large condominium complex you're interested in getting a contract for maintaining. You know she's the decision maker, and you've already walked the complex on your own and made your list. As you walk around the complex with Mary, be sure to listen closely to any suggestions she has, as well as injecting your own, and agree to incorporate her desires into the final plan whenever reasonable.

If you're new at the commercial game, be prepared to answer questions about why you haven't had any commercial experience and why you think you're qualified for it. Answer honestly. If it's because you wanted to develop a strong expertise in landscape principles and practices on a smaller scale first, that's a great answer. Just think about what kind of impression you'd make saying, "I just got my business license yesterday and I came right over!"

Resist the temptation to badmouth whoever was supposedly maintaining the property up until now. It might just be a personal friend of Mary for all you know. If that's the case, she probably feels bad enough letting the person go without having to hear 101 reasons why she shouldn't have hired them in the first place.

At some point, you'll need to talk price. Make sure you don't undercut yourself. Always charge what you need to cover your expenses (including your salary) and make a profit.

Keep the discussion upbeat. Convince Mary to look at the glass half-full. Tell her what you can offer and how you'll go about doing it. If the preliminary list you designed ahead of time still looks doable, hand it to her along with a copy of your resume and a business card before you leave.

If, however, you've discovered that there needs to be significant changes made after the walk-through with Mary, you should tell her you'll incorporate her ideas into the plan and schedule a time you can hand-deliver it later that week, preferably when she's there.

In either case, before you leave, if you're still interested in pursuing the project, show some enthusiasm. Ask about a start date and mention how eager you are to get to work. If you suspect some hesitancy, don't push it, but extend your hand, offer a sincere thank you and follow up with a letter the next day.

If you don't hear back within a week, follow up with a phone call. If after all this, you still don't get the job, you did gain some valuable experience, and you never know what referrals you might still get.

Even if bids are eventually sought (see the section below on bidding), you'll have a head start by being personally acquainted with the decision-maker and will have left a favorable impression. Even if your bid comes in a little higher than the client planned on paying, you might just get the job anyway. Without this personal contact, your bid could have easily ended up in the reject pile.

6.3.2   The Bidding Process

While commercial markets don't always go with the lowest bid, they often do. The industry is constantly trying to change this, and due to lawsuits in specialty areas like pruning and irrigation design, progress is finally being made.

Topping trees is a common practice with lowball bidders, as is the design of poorly put-together irrigation systems. When a two-ton tree branch falls on a vehicle or, worse yet, a person, the court costs can be exorbitant — much higher than had the company originally opted for choosing credentials and professionalism over inferior work for a lower price.

If the project goes out for bid, you may not get it if the decision-maker goes with the lowest bid. Be glad! As mentioned, often when you hand-pick projects you may be able to avoid playing the bidding game altogether and just get hired. Referrals from your residential clients often give you a direct link to the decision-maker, too.

Avoid the tendency to try to win the contract at almost any cost. Winning the bidding war can actually mean losing! The adrenaline rush soon wears off and you're stuck with more than you bargained for. And, because you're bound by a contract, there's not a lot you can do about getting out of it.

I can't tell you how many times an experienced landscape company owner just shakes his or her head and walks away astonished when they see the amount of the awarded bid (incidentally, always request to see this paperwork; government agencies are required to disclose this information). They're not walking away because they're all that disappointed. It's more that they feel pity for the poor person who got it! They know he or she is in some really deep water.

What's an RFP?

RFP stands for Request for Proposal. It's the way the government and some commercial firms advertise their need for any number of types of work. In this case, of course, we'll stick to the need for a company to provide landscaping or related services.

There are many online sites where you can download current RFPs and do keyword searches. A good way to learn what this is all about is to read through lots of RFPs and get an idea of what kind of work and the scope that's generally called for.

Some RFPs are very specific, calling for licensed irrigation designers and auditors while others are general, and are recruiting lawncare firms who will provide routine services. You can learn a lot from studying these, and even following through to see who got the winning bid and what the price tag was.

Low bidding and losing your shirt is a very common problem, especially for those new to the profession. If you do decide to throw in your hat, write down every single cost, both direct and indirect, and make sure they're all accounted for.

If you can, bid on only the portion of the work that you're really good at. If that's lawncare, great. If you've become a Certified Arborist or irrigation specialist, stick to that. Now is not the time to lie about a skill you really don't have. Remember that bidding involves putting forth a legally binding agreement to provide services at a given rate.

As always, don't feel pressured to take every job you're offered. Think each one through carefully. Does it fit into your business plan? Are related costs in line with expected profit? While these questions are very important to answer for every job, you stand to lose less if you undercharge a residential customer than if you underbid on a hundred-acre commercial site.

6.3.3   Industry Partnerships and Referrals

If you create positive relationships with landscape architects and designers, you'll likely get many referrals from them to their clients needing your services. Architects do no installation (unless they hold a contractor's license) and many designers choose not to, and would rather concentrate on mapping everything out. This is where your professionalism and business-savvy come in. Look for opportunities to network with other professionals!

Come right out and offer your services to professionals who are likely in the market for them. There are likely plenty of them out there who will hire you, since you're the specialist with the skills, labor and equipment to get the job done right. The key is to be genuinely willing to work with architects and designers and earn their trust and respect. They need to know that you'll follow their plan and not alter it to better suit your needs, which often puts the customer in the middle and can spoil what could have been a mutually beneficial partnership between the two of you.

On the other hand, once you become more experienced, you'll likely start seeing elements of a design plan you know could be improved and may even prove problematic in the long run. If you've earned the trust and respect of the designer, he or she will not only welcome your suggestions, but will be glad the problem is caught early. It's a two-way street.

Over time, you'll likely pair up with a few architects and designers you work particularly well with and you'll both reap the benefits: more work, satisfied customers who will agree to be references, and a finished product that will sell itself to everyone who sees it.

Here's a tip to consider as you're becoming established. Approach a designer or two whose work you admire and offer to refer design work to him or her, rather than asking the designer to give you work at this point. This is usually easy to follow through on, since many potential clients who have you out to discuss work assume you'll also come up with any designs that are needed yourself.

This can be a very powerful tool to get your foot in the door with high-end professionals who you were reluctant to approach initially. By this time, you will have developed an excellent reputation with a growing client base willing to provide strong references.

Architects and designers prefer not to have competition from contractors who jump into the design game and tend to undercut their prices, which is another reason they often welcome the opportunity to work with you. In this case, each of you sticks to your area of expertise.

6.3.4　Government Contracts

As you become more experienced running your landscape company, you may want to try your hand at procuring a government contract. There is no shortage of money out there — the Department of the Interior and the Agriculture Department are in the top ten government agencies as far as government contracts with small businesses go. In fact, a goal of the federal government is to purchase 25% of their goods and services from small businesses.

I should tell you now that if you don't have access to a computer and the access to Internet, you won't be able to do this kind of work with the federal government. It's required thanks to the Government Paperwork Elimination Act of 1995. I'm not kidding!

While these projects are lucrative, you'll need to spend quite a lot of time writing proposals in response to RFPs, which include an executive summary, how you'll perform and manage the specified duties and, of course, your resume. Also, the government is the government, and frequent reports are required (all submitted online), as well as proof that you have a quality insurance program in place.

You'll definitely get paid, but you may have to wait a while, and it will be on the government's terms, not yours. Sometimes you can set up the contract to allow you to be paid incrementally. This is more likely to happen if you're involved in a large project that will take several months to complete.

If you're in financial straits, a government contract won't save you, but it can level the ebb and flow of a seasonal business like the landscape profession. While there's a lot of money out there to be had, the profit margin isn't much different than a normal commercial contract you would bid for.

Types of work you might provide are erosion control and ecological restoration as well as general landscape maintenance at places like Department of Veterans Affair cemeteries and at National Park Service properties.

To check out active procurement notices, check out the links below:

- *Federal Business Opportunities*
  (Click on "Find Business Opportunities")
  www.fbo.gov

- *GovCB.com*
  www.govcb.com

For help with the art of the bid, contact your local Procurement Technical Assistance Center (PTAC) at **www.aptac-us.org/new**. There are several offices in each state and their services are free to small businesses.

7. Conclusion

You've reached the end of the *FabJob Guide to Become a Landscape Company Owner*. I hope that you are eager and confident about what awaits you in your exciting new career. The rewards and beauty of landscaping are endless. The fruits of your labor will be appreciated for generations to come. You will be actively participating in improving the environment by nurturing and caring for plants that provide oxygen to keep us alive.

To break into the profession, you now know that you don't need a college degree. From reading this book, you have already learned quite a bit about basic landscape principles and how plants grow and function. You know where to go to acquire additional credible information on landscape plants and their care.

It's a really good idea to read one or two of the recommended books in chapter 3, and join a green industry association or two. The industry associations offer a wealth of information about important educational events, what steps to take to provide input on important legislative decisions affecting the green industry. Many even offer live online forums where you can communicate with other landscape professionals about equipment, tools, tricks of the trade, and success stories.

You'll likely want to gain industry experience by working for a year or two for a reputable firm, learning the ins and outs of the business before you dive in independently. This will also give you a chance to begin to develop your own reputation as someone who is a diligent, hardworking and motivated professional. Valuable suggestions for following this course have been presented in this guide.

By now you are well on your way to designing your own vision of the perfect career in horticulture as a landscape company owner. Delve into whatever you choose with passion. I wish you success in your new career, and welcome you into the fascinating world of plants and their care.

7.1 Cooperative Extension Contacts

Take advantage of the hundreds of free and low-cost publications on all aspects of landscape maintenance, including plant selection, irrigation, fertilization, and pest management.

Alabama

Address: Alabama Cooperative Extension System
122 Duncan Hall Annex
Auburn University, AL 36849

Phone: (334) 844-5697

Website: **www.aces.edu/publications**

Alaska

Address: University of Alaska
Fairbanks Cooperative Extension Communications Center
P.O. Box 756180
Fairbanks, AK 99775-6180

Phone: (907) 474-5211

Website: **www.uaf.edu/ces/pubs/**

Arizona

Address: University of Arizona Cooperative Extension
             CALSmart
             4042 N. Campbell Avenue
             Tucson, AZ 85719-1111

Phone: (520) 318-7275
             1 (877) 763-5315 (toll-free)

Website: **http://cals.arizona.edu/pubs**

Arkansas

Address: University of Arkansas Division of Agriculture
             Cooperative Extension Service
             2301 South University Avenue
             Little Rock, AR 72204

Phone: (501) 671-2000

Website: **www.uaex.edu/Other_Areas/publications/default.asp**

California

Address: ANR Communication Services
             6701 San Pablo Ave.
             Oakland, CA 94608

Phone: (510) 642-2431
             1 (800) 994-8849 (toll-free)

Website: **http://ucanr.org/pubs.cfm**

Colorado

Address: Colorado State University
             Cooperative Extension Resource Center (CERC)
             115 General Services Building
             Ft. Collins, CO 80524

Phone: (970) 491-6198
             1 (877) 692-9358 (toll-free)

Website: **www.ext.colostate.edu/pubs/pubs.html**

Connecticut

Address: Home and Garden Education Center
               Ratcliffe Hicks Building (Room 4)
               1380 Storrs Road, Unit 4115
               Storrs, CT 06269-4115

Phone: (860) 486-6271
               1 (877) 486-6271 (toll-free)

Website: **www.ladybug.uconn.edu**

Delaware

Address: Delaware State University Cooperative Extension
               Ulysses S. Washington Center
               1200 N. DuPont Highway
               Dover, DE 19901-2227

Phone: (302) 857-6462

Website: **http://ag.udel.edu/extension/index.php**

Florida

Address: University of Florida (IFAS)UF/IFAS Extension Bookstore
               440 Mowry Road
               PO Box 110011
               Gainesville, FL 32611

Phone: (352) 392-1764

Website: **www.ifasbooks.ufl.edu/merchant2**

Georgia

Address: University of Georgia Cooperative Extension Service
               Ag Business Office
               Room 215, Conner Hall
               Athens, GA 30602

Phone: (706) 542-8999

Website: **www.caes.uga.edu/publications**

Hawaii

Address:	University of Hawaii Cooperative Extension – Communication Services 3050 Maile Way Gilmore 119 Honolulu, HI 96822
Phone:	(808) 956-7036
Website:	**www.ctahr.hawaii.edu/ctahr2001/PIO/FreePubs.asp**

Idaho

Address:	University of Idaho Extension Publications College of Agricultural and Life Sciences P.O. Box 442240 Moscow, ID 83844-2240
Phone:	(208) 885-7982
Website:	**http://info.ag.uidaho.edu/Catalog/catalog.html**

Illinois

Address:	University of Illinois Extension Publications 1917 S. Wright St. Champaign, IL 61820
Phone:	1 (800) 345-6087 (toll-free)
Website:	**http://web.extension.uiuc.edu/state/publications.html**

Indiana

Address:	Purdue University Media Distribution Center 231 S. University Street West Lafayette, IN 47907
Phone:	1 (888) 398-4636
Website:	**www.extension.purdue.edu/extsite/consumer_horticulture.shtml**

Iowa

Address:	Iowa State University Extension Service 119 Printing and Publications Bldg. Ames, IA 50011-3171
Phone:	(515) 294-5247
Website:	**www.extension.iastate.edu/store**

Kansas

Address:	Kansas State University Extension Production Services 24 Umberger Hall Manhattan, KS 66506-3402
Phone:	(785) 532-5830 (10 or fewer titles by phone)
Website:	**www.oznet.ksu.edu/library/**

Kentucky

Address:	University of Kentucky Agricultural Communications Services 131 Scovell Hall Lexington, KY 40546-0064
Phone:	(859) 257-4736
Website:	**www.ca.uky.edu/agc/pubs/pubs.htm**

Louisiana

Address:	LSU Agcenter Communications P.O. Box 25100 Baton Rouge, LA 70894-5100
Phone:	(225) 578-2263
Website:	**www.agctr.lsu.edu/en/communications/publications/**

Maine

Address:	University of Maine Cooperative Extension 5741 Libby Hall, Room 114 Orono, ME 04469-5741
Phone:	(207) 581-3792
Website:	**http://extensionpubs.umext.maine.edu**

Maryland

Address: University of Maryland
AGNR Publications
Room 0300 Symons Hall, Bldg 076
College Park, MD 20742

Phone: Phone the Cooperative Extension office in your county if
you need to order priced publications. Free publications
are listed on the website below.

Website: **http://pubs.agnr.umd.edu**

Massachusetts

Address: UMass Extension Communications & Marketing
40 Campus Center Way
University of Massachusetts
Amherst, MA 01003-9244

Phone: (413) 545-2716

Website: **www.umassturf.org/publications/publications.html**

Michigan

Address: Michigan State University Extension
MSU Bulletin Office
117 Central Services
East Lansing, MI 48824-1001

Phone: (517) 353-6740

Website: **www.msue.msu.edu/portal**

Minnesota

Address: University of Minnesota Extension Service
Extension Distribution Center
405 Coffey Hall
1420 Eckles Ave
St. Paul, MN 55108-6068

Phone: 1 (800) 876-8636

Website: **www.sustland.umn.edu/index.html**

Mississippi

Address: Mississippi State Extension Service
Box 9800
Mississippi State, MS 39762

Phone: Phone the Cooperative Extension office in your county if you need to order priced publications. Free publications are listed on the website below.

Website: **http://msucares.com/lawn/index.html**

Missouri

Address: University of Missouri Cooperative Extension
MU Extension Publications
2800 Maguire Blvd.
Columbia, MO 65211

Phone: (573) 882-7216
1 (800) 292-0969 (toll-free)

Website: **http://extension.missouri.edu/explore/**

Montana

Address: Montana State University Cooperative Extension
Extension Publications
MSU P.O. Box 172040
Bozeman, MT 59717-2040

Phone: (406) 994-3273

Website: **www.montana.edu/wwwpb/pubs/index.html**

Nebraska

Address: University of Nebraska Cooperative Extension
Extension Publications
Box 830918
Lincoln, NE 68583-0918

Phone: Phone the Cooperative Extension office in your county if you need to order priced publications. Free publications are listed on the website below.

Website: **www.ianrpubs.unl.edu/epublic/pages/index.jsp**

Nevada

Address:	University of Nevada, Reno Cooperative Extension Mail Stop 404 Reno, NV 89557-0106
Phone:	Contact the Cooperative Extension office in your county if you do not have access to the publication website below.
Website:	**www.unce.unr.edu/publications/**

New Hampshire

Address:	University of New Hampshire Cooperative Extension 59 College Road Taylor Hall Durham, NH 03824-3587
Phone:	1 (877) 398-4769
Website:	**http://ceinfo.unh.edu/FHGEC/FHGEC.htm**

New Jersey

Address:	Cooperative Research & Extension Cook College Rutgers, The State University of New Jersey 88 Lipman Dr. New Brunswick, NJ 08901-8525
Phone:	Contact the Cooperative Extension office in your county if you do not have access to the publication website below.
Website:	**http://njaes.rutgers.edu/ltm/**

New Mexico

Address:	New Mexico State University Cooperative Extension Agricultural Communications Bulletin Office Box 30003, MSC 3AI Las Cruces, NM 88003-8003
Phone:	(505) 646-2701
Website:	**http://cahe.nmsu.edu/pubs/_h**

New York

Address: Cornell University
The Resource Center
P.O. Box 3884
Ithaca, NY 14852-3884

Phone: (607) 255-2080

Website: **http://hosts.cce.cornell.edu/pmep/shop/**

North Carolina

Address: North Carolina State University Publications
Campus Box 7603
Raleigh, NC 27695-7603

Phone: (919) 513-3112

Website: **www.ces.ncsu.edu/Publications/lawngarden.php**

North Dakota

Address: North Dakota State University Extension Service
Distribution Center
Morrill Hall, P.O. Box 5655
Fargo, ND 58105-5655

Phone: (701) 231-7882

Website: **www.ag.ndsu.edu/horticulture/**

Ohio

Address: Ohio State University Extension
Media Distribution
385 Kottman Hall
2021 Coffey Rd.
Columbus, OH 43210-1044

Phone: (614) 292-1607

Website: **http://ohioline.osu.edu**

Oklahoma

Address: Oklahoma State University Cooperative Extension
139 Agriculture Hall
Stillwater, OK 74078

Phone: (405) 744-5398

Website: **http://pods.dasnr.okstate.edu/docushare/dsweb/View/
Collection-389**

Oregon

Address: Oregon State University Cooperative Extension
101 Ballard Hall
Corvallis, OR 97331-3606

Phone: Contact the Cooperative Extension office in your county
if you do not have access to the publication
website below.

Website: **http://extension.oregonstate.edu**

Pennsylvania

Address: Pennsylvania State University
Publications Distribution Center
112 Agricultural Administration Building
University Park, PA 16802-2602

Phone: (405) 744-5398

Website: **http://pubs.cas.psu.edu/Publications.asp**

Rhode Island

Address: Rhode Island Cooperative Extension Education Center
3 East Alumni Ave.
Kingston, RI 02881

Phone: (401) 874-2929
1 (800) 448-1011 (toll-free)

Website: **www.uri.edu/cels/ceoc/**

South Carolina

Address:	Clemson University Cooperative Extension 103 Barre Hall Clemson, SC 29634-0101
Phone:	1 (888) 656-9988
Website:	**http://hgic.clemson.edu/**

South Dakota

Address:	South Dakota State Cooperative Extension ABS Bulletin Room Box 2212A South Dakota State University Brookings, SD 57007
Phone:	(605) 688-5628
Website:	**http://agbiopubs.sdstate.edu**

Tennessee

Address:	University of Tennessee Cooperative Extension 2621 Morgan Circle 121 Morgan Hall Knoxville, TN 37996
Phone:	Contact the Cooperative Extension office in your county if you do not have access to the website below.
Website:	**www.utextension.utk.edu/publications/homeGarden/default.asp**

Texas

Address:	Texas A & M University System Cooperative Extension Publications P.O. Box 1209 Bryan, TX 77806
Phone:	1 (888) 900-2577
Website:	**http://agrilifebookstore.org**

Utah

Address:	Utah State University Cooperative Extension Publications Logan, UT 84322
Phone:	(435) 797-1000
Website:	**http://extension.usu.edu/htm/publications**

Vermont

Address:	University of Vermont Publications Office Adams House 601 Main Street Burlington, VT 05401-3439
Phone:	(802) 656-3131
Website:	**www.uvm.edu/~uvmext/programs/home/default.php**

Virginia

Address:	Virginia Cooperative Extension 110 Hutcheson Hall Virginia Tech Blacksburg, VA 24061
Phone:	Publication orders are only accepted online (below) or from the local Cooperative Extension office in your county.
Website:	**www.ext.vt.edu/resources/anrpublications.html**

Washington

Address:	Washington State University Cooperative Extension Publications P.O. Box 645912 Pullman, WA 99164-5912
Phone:	(509) 335-2857 1 (800) 723-1763 (toll-free)
Website:	**http://pubs.wsu.edu/cgi-bin/pubs/index.html**

West Virginia

Address: West Virginia University Extension Service
507 Knapp Hall
P.O. Box 6031
Morgantown, WV 26506-6031

Phone: (304) 293-4221

Website: **www.wvu.edu/~exten/publications/**

Wisconsin

Address: University of Wisconsin
Cooperative Extension Publications
PO Box 342831
Milwaukee, WI 53234-2831

Phone: 1 (877) 947-7827

Website: **http://learningstore.uwex.edu**

Wyoming

Address: University of Wyoming Cooperative Extension
Ag Resource Center
Department 3313
1000 E. University
Laramie, WY 82071

Phone: (307) 766-2115

Website: **http://ces.uwyo.edu/Pubs.asp**

Save 50% on Your Next Purchase

Would you like to save money on your next FabJob guide purchase? Please contact us at **www.FabJob.com/feedback.asp** to tell us how this guide has helped prepare you for your dream career. If we publish your comments on our website or in our promotional materials, we will send you a gift certificate for 50% off your next purchase of a FabJob guide.

Get Free Career Advice

Get valuable career advice for free by subscribing to the FabJob newsletter. You'll receive insightful tips on: how to break into the job of your dreams or start the business of your dreams, how to avoid career mistakes, and how to increase your on-the-job success. You'll also receive discounts on FabJob guides, and be the first to know about upcoming titles. Subscribe to the FabJob newsletter at **www.FabJob.com/newsletter.asp**.

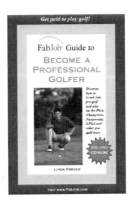

Does Someone You Love Deserve a Dream Career?

Giving a FabJob® guide is a fabulous way to show someone you believe in them and support their dreams. Help them break into the career of their dreams with more than 75 career guides to choose from.

Visit www.FabJob.com to order guides today!

How to Install the CD-ROM

This bonus CD-ROM contains helpful forms and checklists you can revise and use when planning events. It also includes an electronic version of this book, which you can use to quickly connect to the websites we've mentioned (as long as you have access to the Internet and the Acrobat Reader program on your computer).

To install the CD-ROM, these simple steps will work with most computers:

1. Insert the CD-ROM into your computer CD drive.

2. Double click on the "My Computer" icon on your desktop.

3. Double click on the icon for your CD-ROM drive.

4. Read the "Read Me" file on the CD-ROM for more information.